MW00474041

Doing Theological Research

Doing Theological Research

*An Introductory Guide
for Survival in Theological Education*

ROBERT W. PAZMIÑO

WIPF & STOCK · Eugene, Oregon

DOING THEOLOGICAL RESEARCH
An Introductory Guide for Survival in Theological Education

Wipf & Stock
An Imprint of Wipf and Stock Publishers
199 W. 8th Ave., Suite 3
Eugene, OR 97401
www.wipfandstock.com

ISBN 13: 978-1-60608-939-2

Manufactured in the U.S.A.

Unless otherwise stated, Scripture quotations are from the New Revised Standard Version. Please use standard language for this Bible translation.

Dedicated to all my students in theological education,
past, present, and future

Contents

Introduction

STUDENTS IN pursuit of theological education will discover the essentials of conducting theological research in this concise introductory work. It provides an overview of expectations from my twenty-eight years of guiding students with their research and study in a variety of settings and from working with theological faculty in a number of schools.

The three general objectives of the book are:

1. To explore the purposes and basics of theological study and research.

2. To reaffirm the importance of theological study and research in a variety of theological disciplines.

3. To inspire Christians in relation to the calling to study as a form of worship and spiritual discipline.

If readers embrace the passion and potential of theological research this work has accomplished its intent. My hope is that persons called to theological study and research will love God with all of their mind in addition to all of their heart, soul, and strength throughout their journey in this world and the next.

The four appendices of this work include actual teaching guides that my colleagues and I use in our classes to assist students with their research and writing. While I served as the interim dean of the faculty at Andover Newton Theological School students identified these guides as helpful for their learning. I appreciate the willingness of my colleagues to share their wisdom with readers of this guide so that all our efforts in theological education might glorify God. These appendices provide specific insights for research and writing in theological disciplines that are identified in chapter 4.

Where to Start

THEOLOGY LITERALLY means the study of *theos* or God.[1] Theological education extends an exciting invitation to explore the study of God with implications for all of life. The invitation to love God with all of one's mind in graduate-level study also seeks to engage the heart, soul, and body of theological students. This invitation in many cases includes the exploration of one's calling or vocation in life.

Theological education is a spiritual invitation to explore one's own love of God and neighbor. This is realized in community with those who both honor and question the spiritual sources and wells that have and will sustain persons, communities, and societies. Sustenance is found in living spiritual traditions and in the new offerings of God's Spirit to address present and future challenges in the world. Spiritual life and traditions are studied from the perspective of loving critics who daily recognize our human limitations and God's ever-present grace.

Theological education is an intellectual invitation to explore critical and post-critical faith perspectives that pose a challenge for those who are threatened by a movement to closely examine conventional faith understandings. James Fowler considers the stages of individual reflective faith and conjunctive faith that young, middle age, and older adults can encounter on their life

1. Another definition of theology is faith seeking understanding. Such a definition assumes one has faith understood as a relationship with God.

journeys during theological study. Basically, individual reflective faith invites a choice of one's own personal beliefs, values, and commitments within and beyond inherited faith traditions to affirm and own a particular religious identity, especially one that is shared with faith communities.[2] Theological study provides an opportunity to explore theological options from which to choose intentionally. Conjunctive faith integrates life's polarities and mysteries in a both/and perspective and embraces an openness to a diversity of truths and traditions beyond one's own particular faith perspective.[3] Theological study invites students to wrestle with the integration of faith and life. Both these faith stages named by Fowler call for a stretch intellectually and personally for those called to study in community with teachers and fellow students both in and outside the walls of theological schools.

Theological education generally has been organized around a discipline division known as the theological quadrilateral that is comprised of four areas of study: biblical, theological, historical, and practical. In addition, historically a two-fold pattern that interfaces theory and practice is often maintained that combines the academic and professional preparation of theological students. This combination intends for clergy and laity that they be informed, formed, and transformed in ways that enable them to be effective in their callings in the world. These curricular and organizational patterns were identified historically in the mid-twentieth century in a series of theological education studies sponsored by the then American Association of Theological Schools, now the Association of Theological Schools (ATS), the body that accredits theological schools. The Carnegie Foundation also supported the studies, which are commonly known as the

---

2. James W. Fowler, *Becoming Adult, Becoming Christian: Adult Development and Christian Faith* (San Francisco: Jossey-Bass, 2000), 40–60.

3. Ibid.

Niebuhr studies. H. Richard Niebuhr, Daniel Day Williams, and James M. Gustafson write and edit the study reports.[4]

A more recent study also supported by the Carnegie Foundation, *Educating Clergy*, focuses upon preparation for the professions of priest, pastor, and rabbi in particular as the primary, though not exclusive, constituency of theological education.[5] I think that more broadly theological education seeks to engage the head, heart, and hands of persons. It strives to foster the student outcomes of critical and creative theological reflection, spiritual imagination, and transformative practices in a variety of ministries. H. Richard Niebuhr back in the twentieth century hoped that theological education might nurture the love of God and neighbor.[6] I think that Niebuhr's purposes should now be expanded to include God's love of the world (John 3:16) understood as God's creation. This additional purpose is crucial with the global ecological crisis that confronts humanity.

My thoughts up to this point assume one is presently studying or convinced they are to begin theological study. A prior decision requires discernment whether to undertake such a venture. Discerning a call to begin study at a theological school is best considered in conversation with a number of people. First a conversation with those who know you well in your current situation is important to broaden your personal perceptions of what theological study can mean at this point in your life journey. A call to a theological seminary, divinity school, or a graduate program in theology may be distinct from having clarity regard-

---

4. H. Richard Niebuhr, Daniel D. Williams, and James M. Gustafson, *The Advancement of Theological Education* (New York: Harper & Bros., 1957); H. Richard Niebuhr, Daniel D. Williams, and James M. Gustafson, *The Purpose of the Church and Its Ministry* (New York: Harper & Bros., 1956).

5. Charles R. Foster and others, *Educating Clergy: Teaching Practices and Pastoral Imagination* (San Francisco: Jossey-Bass, 2006).

6. Niebuhr, *Purpose of the Church and Its Ministry.*

ing your profession or ministry after your study is completed.[7] For me personally, clarity came two weeks before completing my Master of Divinity program. Either I was going to pastor an urban congregation in Brooklyn, New York, or begin a doctoral program in the area of religious education to prepare for a career in teaching. The financial support to pursue further study was secured close to my day of graduation.

In addition to persons who know you well, for those considering the preparation for particular ministries, such as congregational pastoral ministry, interaction with persons currently leading such work can be valuable in a process of discernment. In my case, persons in both campus ministries whose advice I initially dismissed only heeding them five years later, and persons in my local church provided feedback that I should consider seminary training because of the gifts they identified in my ministries with others. It should be noted that resistance to a call to seminary is not uncommon among those studying at theological schools from my years of teaching experience.

A third group of persons with whom to discuss the possibility of theological education is those currently working and teaching at theological schools. I do recall a letter received from a seminary professor who shared his advice regarding a possible career in Christian counseling that led me to apply to programs in clinical psychology and social work. The advice included the recommendation of a Master of Divinity degree prior to the possible integration of Christian perspectives in counseling or social work at the doctoral level. That advice enabled me to discover and deepen my love for Christian education. For me, Christian education embraced a preventative communal approach to share with persons the resources of their faith in confronting life transitions and crises.

7. One work that helped me in my decision to enter seminary was Edmund P. Clowney, *Called to the Ministry* (Phillipsburg, NJ: Presbyterian and Reformed Publishing, 1964).

Beyond these three groups of persons, those considering theological education are wise to pray about their decision and be in communion with God who is both the subject and object of theological study. Such a suggestion calls for spiritual discernment along with an open heart and mind to be surprised by joy in the act of seeking a full and faithful life in service to God, neighbors, and the world.

2

The Five Commandments of Theological Research

Readers should be delighted that there are not Ten Commandments to recall in considering the challenging task of theological research that is at the heart of theological education. These five commandments need to be applied to distinct theological disciplines that are the topic of chapter 4, but they provide a helpful overview of the basic expectations that are operative in theological study and research. The naming of these commandments is not original to me, but was passed on by Max Stackhouse who served as a colleague and mentor when I first joined the faculty of Andover Newton Theological School in 1986. The commentary or midrash on Max's five commandments are my elaborations upon the oral tradition I received and are offered to initiate novices to the wonders and challenges of theological study that can be seen as a form of worship.

The five commandments as passed on to me:

1. If it is not theological, it is not deep

2. Wrestle an angel

3. Pick a prism

4. Tell the truth, warts and all

5. Read, formulate, talk, read, and reformulate

Here is my midrash on Max's commandments.

1. IF IT IS NOT THEOLOGICAL, IT IS NOT DEEP

This is the academic equivalent of the first commandment of the Jewish Scriptures: "You shall have no other gods before me" (Exod 20:3; Deut 5:7). Or it is first of the great commandments noted in the Christian Scriptures: "You shall love the Lord your God with all of your heart, soul, *mind*, and strength" (Mark 12:30; Luke 10:27; Matt 22:37). Theology helps to move us beyond our immediate context to address matters of continuing significance and depth. In a theological school, theology is still the queen of the sciences. Theologies vary, but the awareness of our theological traditions and the implicit theologies in our work is foundational to theological study and research. For example every psychology or psychological school embraces an implicit theological anthropology. A theological anthropology is an understanding about persons and their origin, disposition, need, makeup, and ultimate destiny that proposes values or virtues to guide human life.

2. WRESTLE AN ANGEL

This second commandment is to choose something to study or research that can potentially wound us. Another way of saying this comes from Abraham Heschel who noted that "religion begins with a question, and theology with a problem."[1] Addressing real and deeply felt questions and problems involves taking a risk like wrestling with an angel as described in Genesis 32:22–32. In this account Jacob is at a major point of transition in his life as he returns home to encounter his estranged brother Esau. He is alone the night before the encounter having sent his family ahead. Jacob is dealing with a number of contending forces and

1. Reuven Kimelman, "Abraham Joshua Heschel: Our Generation's Teacher in Honor of the Tenth Yahrzeit," *Religion and Intellectual Life* 2 (Winter 1985): 17.

fears in his life. Just as conflicting spiritual and moral forces and certain negative forces impact Jacob, they inhibit all persons, groups, families, communities, and the very social and structural fabric of our lives. The task in wrestling may be to name the destroyers of life, life as God intended it to be lived in fullness and joy even amid suffering. Naming, opposing, and contending with the destroyers of life is risky, but certain positive forces hold promise for renewal, restoration, and hope in our personal and corporate lives. Jacob wrestled with an angel and was touched at the point of his greatest strength—his hip or groin. He had a history of running, but he could no longer run after wrestling with the angel of the Lord. This commandment requires us in theological research to be vulnerable enough to expose our strengths and see if they need to be transformed remembering the watchword of the Reformation (both Protestant and Catholic Reformations) *semper reformanda*, always being reformed by the gracious working of God's Spirit in human life, including the life of study in theological education.

3. PICK A PRISM

One cannot do everything in one paper, presentation, or project in theological study or in any other area of academic work. Therefore the need is to select and narrow down one's topic, question, problem, or issue for research. A prism serves to focus one or more streams of light at one focal point. That focal point needs to be clearly identified in one's writing or presentation. But prisms also serve to divide the light into diverse and wondrous colors that can be elaborated upon in the implications of one's research or the conclusions drawn from the study.[2] The clear focus at the focal point serves to draw out the multiple impli-

2. One practical suggestion is to note insights in the content footnotes or subtext of one's academic writing to allow for an even flow in the text itself.

cations and applications of one's work. With a prism one must turn the angles to get the maximum effect that suggests the need to reconfigure a question, problem, issue, or thesis statement to gain the best possible perception and perspective. One example comes from the work of a student who wanted to explore the spirituality of pastors drawing upon distinct denominational spiritual traditions that came into better focus when the topic shifted to consider laity instead of clergy.

hard piece of skin

4. TELL THE TRUTH, WARTS AND ALL

This commandment relates to one of the actual Ten Commandments, the ninth commandment in particular: "Do not bear false witness" (Exod 20:16; Deut 5:20). Given the bent of persons to be successful or to appear competent, this results in the tendency not to confront the place of failure. We are tempted to name areas or results not confirmed or warranted by the findings of our research. Theological research calls us to share honestly our findings. The human situation involves paradox and inconsistency. The surd factor or dysfunctional patterns affect reality that needs to be identified. It is appropriate to state additional work that needs to be done or new questions that arise in the process of research.

Contrary

5. READ, FORMULATE, TALK, READ, AND REFORMULATE

This fifth and final commandment suggests that good work requires a process. I only knew one person who could formulate final drafts of his writing on the first try and I ended up studying his life and ministry for my doctoral research. Compared to precomputer days, the process of refining and developing work is immensely facilitated by computer technology assuming that adequate time has been allotted for this important process. The process of refining work requires perseverance and a willingness to receive constructive feedback from others. Developing habits of reviewing work and allowing others to respond can greatly improve the quality of work where "Iron sharpens iron, and one person sharpens the wits of another" (Prov 27:17). Limits, of course, must be recognized in the refining process and the encouragement to remember is not to lose heart or avoid the edification possible with constructive feedback. Theological study and research is worth the best efforts in making a lasting contribution personally and professionally in the present and future.

Beyond following the five commandments, students can situate their study and research by using three additional approaches that can be experienced as less intimidating. These three approaches include: first, a move from experience to expertise; second, an examination of one's sources; and third, the discernment of meaning in one's research. Therefore, along with the observation of the five commandments, four possible ways are suggested for students to engage theological research with fruitful results.

MOVE FROM EXPERIENCE TO EXPERTISE

The importance of personal experience is honored in narrative approaches to theology and ministry. Christian faith honors history and narrative. But in an age of experience, the challenge in theological study is to move to informed and examined experience or relative expertise, at least enough expertise to perform well academically. In this second way to engage theological study, the place to begin is to relate one's work to a community of discourse or to be in dialogue with others not only in person, but with those you encounter through your study. One proviso is to engage those with whom one disagrees on a particular question, issue, or topic. Next, students are encouraged to speak to a specific audience in one's work so that clarity can emerge. Most often the audience is one's professor or instructor and possibly one's peers, but with prior agreement with a professor another wider audience can be creatively addressed. A third step is to provide a reflective perspective that is critical to the theological setting by drawing upon theological understanding to assess one's experience. Personal experience must be expanded upon to include authoritative texts like the Scriptures, various traditions in one's setting, and reasoned inquiry. Authoritative texts can include the Bible or other documents that guide the life of religious communities. Texts are subject to interpretation. Traditions can be denominational, theological, historical, and cultural patterns and practices that become living when reappropriated in contemporary settings. Traditions are subject to both affirmation and critique. Reasoned inquiry calls for a comprehensive and systematic handling of questions that explores assumptions and presuppositions brought to one's study.

EXAMINE YOUR SOURCES

Initially a theological student asks what authorities and sources are essential in the area of one's topic. In relation to authoritative voices, a student considers upon whom those sources themselves are drawing. This examination can lead to the questioning and critique of those sources. Theological scholars often begin this work by looking at the footnotes or endnotes of the works one is exploring or using. This encourages an intellectual curiosity to trace ideas back to their origins or foundations even during a time when anti-foundational sentiments exist in postmodern thinking.

This examination can begin to identify various voices in a field of study or in relation to a particular topic, question, or issue with a possible contention in play. In relation to a theological discipline the question is often what paradigms are dominant and what are marginal? A paradigm is a dominant framework that guides all thought and practice, but it is important to note that paradigms undergo shifts over time.

In addition to paradigms, *model* methodologies are used to guide the research. Students can inquire which methodologies are acceptable in one's field of inquiry or even what alternatives can be suggested. Every methodology as with every paradigm has its strengths and weaknesses. Often the most creative scholarship is interdisciplinary or multidisciplinary in character and can also be autobiographical in drawing upon the wells of experience.

In practical theological disciplines the social sciences are often drawn upon. In the social sciences a distinction is often made between quantitative and qualitative methods. Quantitative methods involve counting and analyzing using correlational, experimental, and empirical approaches. Qualitative methods see the whole, the gestalt, and explore intentionality, interpretation, and interaction. The distinction is often made that quantitative methods stress objectivity, whereas qualitative methods include subjectivity along with objectivity.

DISCERN MEANING

The three prior ways to approach theological research seek to find meaning, but each way has its promises and problems in disclosing truth or in discovering knowledge. In the theological disciplines there are various ways of knowing and several canons for exploring knowledge. The challenge in theological study within the Christian tradition is that knowledge is affirmed on two levels. Supernatural or spiritual knowledge through revelation is affirmed. Natural knowledge through reason is also affirmed. Theology wrestles with the interplay of supernatural knowledge and natural knowledge and sits at the crossroads of revelation and reason. Christian faith has also affirmed that God is both rational and knowable and God is irrational or at least nonrational as bathed in mystery. The search for theological meaning embraces this paradox.

At this juncture or crossroads of revelation and reason, the religious traditions of Judaism and Christianity can help the theological student by drawing upon the insights of one of my professors, Philip Phenix. Professor Phenix proposed that religious traditions provide meaning by focusing on various elements of religious life. The danger of his analysis is that it tends to reduce the fullness of any tradition that needs to be seen as multidimensional. Nevertheless, Phenix's insights can provide entry points for the exploration of meaning. Protestantism stresses beliefs, doctrines, and creeds to provide meaning through the intellectual, rational, and doctrinal dimensions of faith. Eastern Orthodoxy stresses rites and rituals to provide meaning through the aesthetic and sacramental dimensions of faith. Judaism stresses codes, practices, and laws to honor meaning through the ethical, intentional, and moral dimensions of faith. Roman Catholicism stresses organizations, structures, and institutions to provide meaning through the corporate and societal dimensions of faith.[3] I would add to Professor Phenix's analysis the religious tradition of Pentecostalism and Charismatic Renewal. This tradition stresses relationships and community to honor meaning through the mystical and spiritual dimensions of faith. Each religious tradition has incorporated the various dimensions of faith named, but the relative stress upon certain dimensions can serve as a point of distinction for the discernment of meaning. For theological students the panorama of meaning-making is open while recognizing the particular gifts within each religious tradition and how new insights are gained across traditions and in recovering what may be forgotten.

3. Philip Phenix, lecture October 10, 1979, at Teachers College, Columbia University, New York, New York for the course "Education and the Faiths of Mankind."

To complement Phenix's analysis of religious traditions, his categories for six realms of meaning can assist theological students in orienting their study and research in relation to the academic world and its search for meaning.[4] These six realms of meaning can be drawn upon to gain understanding and discernment in study:

1. Symbolics—provide symbol systems through language, rituals, mathematics, and the careful use of language with clear definitions. Language study has particular importance in biblical study. Symbols have importance for the study of worship or liturgy and the arts including the arts of ministry. Theological study requires the acquisition of new language. Terms such as exegesis and theological reflection call for definition and understanding.

2. Empirics—draw upon empirical data and the use of the *base on Observation also* scientific method with controls, disprovability, and disconfirmability involved. Those theological disciplines like the areas of ethics and practical theology that draw upon the social and physical sciences make use of empirics.

3. Aesthetics—engage arts, imagination, and creativity. Increased interest in theology and the arts has emerged in theological education over the past twenty years.

4. Synoetics—honors direct, personal experience and the I-Thou encounter with relational insights, intuition, and existential assurance affirmed. The area of spiritual formation considered in chapter 6 has become more central to theological education as a result of cultural and societal shifts.

5. Ethics—questions obligation, responsibility, and accountability in all areas of life honoring morality and goodness

4. See Philip H. Phenix, *Realms of Meaning: A Philosophy of the Curriculum for General Education* (New York: McGraw-Hill, 1964).

in personal and social life. Personal, professional, and social ethics are key areas for theological study that affect life in the church and world where faith finds expression.

6. Synoptics—provide an overall sense of a pattern, a comprehensive and integrated sense of the whole that enables one to see the connections. Beyond the synoptic issue in the New Testament study of the Gospels, theology strives to provide a comprehensive sense of the whole of life with God.

Theological study draws upon these realms of meaning in conversation with religious traditions to share knowledge and wisdom required for faithful living today and in the future. The realms are engaged distinctly in theological disciplines but the perennial questions persist that are explored in chapter 3. Perennial questions serve to integrate insights across religious traditions and realms of academic meaning.

3

Perennial Questions

THEOLOGICAL STUDY and research in many ways follows a pattern of human and intellectual inquiry that began in creation with the ability to question reality. Speaking of the creation, its description in the book of Genesis is helpful before exploring the perennial questions in human inquiry:

> In the beginning when God created the heavens and the earth, the earth was a formless void and darkness covered the face of the deep, while a wind from God swept over the face of the waters. Then God said, "Let there be light"; and there was light. And God saw that the light was good; and God separated the light from the darkness. God called the light Day, and the darkness he called Night. And there was evening and there was morning, the first day (Gen 1:1–5).

This description has insights for the recreation and repair of the world that is one of the fruits of theological study and research. This passage notes the formless void and darkness covering the face of the deep with a wind sweeping over the face of the waters. Study of the universe has found the presence of light matter, dark matter, and holes in space. Such descriptors capture the feeling of students who confront a body of content and the course tasks of theological disciplines new to them. The descriptors capture the challenge of the creative process like holding in one's hands a lump of unformed and pliable clay that needs shaping definition.

The process of creation in theological study involves light and darkness as noted here in Genesis and both light and darkness are needed to gain both visual and theological perspective. There is a beauty of the evening and morning, of the night and the day, hopefully not burdened with too many all-nighters for the completion of papers and presentations for seminary courses. Creation as suggested in Genesis involves both ardor and order to make meaning. Ardor or passion is found in the formless void from the deep and in the wind as it sweeps over the dynamic waters of life. Order is found in the calling forth of the light and in the seeing and setting of patterns such as day and night. The combination of light and darkness, of order and ardor, are possible in theological research that honors the reality that theological students are created creative and can share their creativity through their work.

One way to provide form to theological research is to attend to the perennial questions of human inquiry. The playful handling of these questions can add ardor to the order suggested by responding to questions recalling Abraham Heschel's insight that "religion begins with a question, and theology with a problem." The perennial questions are ones that a good investigative reporter typically asks making use of interrogative pronouns—what, why, where, how, when and who. In raising these questions, inquirers hope to create a web of meaning. Each of these perennial questions will be explored with implications for theological research.

WHAT?

By first considering the *what* question, students are called to clarity of focus, direction, and topic in the particular area of their research. What do you want to study and write about? What do you want to do? Clarity with regard to the content and nature of one's research, one's work, and one's specific study is crucial to guide one's efforts. It takes time and effort to gain clarity along with conversation with others so that what one is clear about can actually be communicated with others. A playful handling with *what* can consider *so what?* Or, *what if?* Considering *what if* can help foster the creative juices to flow while engaging the imagination beyond past and present realities. Liturgy itself can be seen as the playful work of the people of God in public worship. Theological study and research can actually be seen as a form of worship that seeks to glorify and enjoy God through the exercise of one's mind and skill in expression and dialogue.

WHY?

By considering *why* theological inquirers explore the purposes, intentions, goals, and outcomes of their work. The oft repeated inquiry from children or youth can apply: Why bother? For theological students the questions may be posed differently: Why do you want to do this or study this? What purposes or goals are you addressing or wrestling with in your work? Theological study and research is work that requires discipline and imagination. Tapping into personal and/or communal motivations and purposes is crucial to sustain work over time.

Parker Palmer in analyzing the interests or motivations for learning within education identifies control, curiosity, or compassion.[1] All three may be operative with mixed motives a reality in human life and inquiry, but the Apostle Paul reflects on the motive of compassion or love that can be related to the real sacrifices to acquire knowledge in theological study in particular and any study in general:

> Now concerning food sacrificed to idols: we know that
> "all of us possess knowledge." Knowledge puffs up, but
> love builds up. Anyone who claims to know something

1. Parker J. Palmer, *To Know As We Are Known: A Spirituality of Education* (San Francisco: Harper & Row, 1983), 7–8.

does not yet have the necessary knowledge, but anyone
who loves God is known by him (1 Cor 8:1–3).

Paul's suggests that knowledge motivated by love builds up
or edifies and that one's love of God is an essential foundation
for the pursuit of knowledge that is possible in theological education. Beyond any information or knowledge is understanding
and wisdom that have connections with spiritual life and one's
love of God. In his work *Spiritual Life*, John Westerhoff defines
spiritual life as a "love affair with God."[2] Using Westerhoff's definition, one ultimate purpose of theological study poses a question for anyone who engages such work: "How is your love life
with God?" If theology is the study of God, one result of that
study is a deepening of knowledge of God leading hopefully to
an enhanced love life with God fostered by that study. Therefore
one ultimate answer to the *why* of theological research can consider the deepening love of God, neighbor, and all of creation.
This is not to exclude a place for both curiosity and control as
interests related to the *why* question. Nevertheless the interest of
compassion or love holds the greatest potential in guiding and
fulfilling the purpose of theological study and research.

A playful handling of the *why* question leads us to ask *why
not?* Senator Robert Kennedy is remembered for his words: "Some
persons see what is and ask why? Others dream what can be and
ask why not?" By asking *why not* persons explore imaginatively
the possibilities of change, reform, transformation, and revolu-
tion. Theological education fosters the exploration of ideals and
hopes beyond the realities confronted. W. E. B. Du Bois in his
philosophy of education, observed that education is a "necessary
combination of the permanent and the contingent—of the ideal
and the practical in workable equilibrium—(and this) must be in
every age and place, a matter of infinite experiment and frequent

2. John H. Westerhoff, *Spiritual Life: The Foundation for Preaching
and Teaching* (Louisville: Westminster John Knox, 1994), 1.

mistakes."[3] At its best, theological education enables students to embrace ideals and dream about practical expressions of those ideals as they are brought into reality through transformative practices by asking *why not?*

WHERE?

This question considers where one locates a particular work in the universe of possibilities and in relation to the work of others. The context for one's work makes all the difference and stating it clearly sets the stage or describes the setting for one's work with the hope that insights or perspectives or principles might illumine others and transfer with appropriate provisos to other settings. The naming of one's context calls for clarity with regard to limits and the identification of one's social location. These factors affect the perspective assumed by the researcher. Postmodern sensitivities require sensitivity to the potential power dynamics of social location and the real limits of claims of objectivity based upon personal and communal affiliations. The naming of assumptions and limitations based upon one's setting and the scope of one's vision for the study and research is a form of intellectual honesty that can foster dialogue.

A playful handling of the *where* question can propose the following: Where in the world am I in relation to this topic, question, or issue? Where in the world can what I propose be possible or desirable? Where in the world can this become a reality and for whom? These questions may lead to direct and concrete grounding and application as well as imaginative proposals for application in a variety of life and ministry settings.

3. W. E. B. Du Bois, *The Souls of Black Folk* (New York: Bantam Books, 1989), 65. Chapter 6 of this work that is entitled "Of the Training of Black Men" articulates Du Bois's remarkable educational philosophy.

Related to practice

HOW?

The *how* question is of particular appeal to persons with a practical or pragmatic bent, but more generally in areas of study and research relates to questions of methods of inquiry. A student can ask, "How will I approach, conduct, validate, and evaluate my work or my study?" The choice of methods or research approaches engaged, and if multiple methods are used the coherence of the methods, are important issues for what one discovers or discloses. Various methods are used in theological study including social science methods (qualitative and quantitative), empirical, archival, historical, philosophical, biblical, and theological methods to name general categories. The need for greater specificity within each theological discipline is explored in the next chapter.

The assumption in a theological school is that students will relate their work to theological and in many cases biblical or other traditional and authoritative sources to provide warrants for their insights. The drawing upon various methods and authoritative sources for knowledge requires critical appropriation. In other words, theological students need to critically draw upon theological traditions and content along with their experience and reason in the methods used to discover and disclose truth and wisdom. In an experiential age, the need is for informed and examined experience. Biblical, theological, historical, ethical, and practical traditions and current perspectives inform personal and corporate experiences in Christian practice. In addition, the claims of experience are examined by reason and in communication with others to discern truth and embrace wisdom issuing in abundant life. The particular challenge in theological study is the exploration of the connection between reason and revelation that is a life long task.

A playful handling of *how* can consider how is it possible to say this or see this based upon the methods or modes of inquiry selected. It can be noted that some of the most creative theological work emerges from interdisciplinary or multidisciplinary work that often includes autobiographical connections. This observation honors the important place of experience without succumbing to the dangers of uninformed and unexamined experience that can typify some work at the graduate level. My experience and perspectives processed through the screens of biblical, theological, historical, and ethical traditions may have resonance with others and serve to disclose some wisdom along their path.

WHEN?

This question considers the timing of the particular study or research both for the student and the scope of the inquiry itself. The work requires clarity regarding the historical, psychological, sociological, cultural, and socioeconomic boundaries. A work is being done at a particular time in one's personal and communal history. A theological student can consider: What hints do you gain from the timing of your inquiry? What about the readiness of others to hear, consider, or receive that which you are saying or writing on this topic? Risks are inevitable in any effort or expression and one's readers may be hearing and responding to different facets of one's work. In terms of the response of one's professors, peers, or other readers, those who share their work as required can consider: Am I ready to receive constructive criticism and feedback? A vulnerability and openness is needed, but risks are taken in any venture to express one's self on various topics, and the risks are worth taking.

A playful handling of *when* can ask: When might others hear and respond to our thoughts and feelings shared in our work? In one sense there is no good time for destructive critique, but constructive critique can foster communication and facilitate dialogue and mutual edification.

WHO?

One immediate question to consider is who is our audience? In other words, for whom are you writing, recounting, or sharing your work? Yet another way to consider this question is: What relationships can be fostered as a result of your work? This last question intends to extend the circles of communication and relationship. There is the obvious relationship with one's professor(s) or instructor(s), but one can consider peers and various communities of discourse depending upon the area of one's work. In addition many works are shared through the electronic community of Internet globally. Issues of confidentiality and trust are at stake in broadening one's audience, but a wider consideration of publics beyond one's immediate context is worthwhile.

A playful handling of *who* can be posed: Who can be invited to hear, read, or observe what you have discovered or disclosed? Who can come to the table as you share your findings? Who cares? The matter of care is important if the interest of compassion or love has launched the inquiry from its inception following the insights of both the Apostle Paul and Parker Palmer.

CONCLUSION

No doubt other questions can be posed in responding to theological study and research, some of which relate to the specific theological discipline engaged and the questions each one of us bring from our life journey. Nevertheless, these perennial questions are addressed either explicitly or implicitly in theological research and can be drawn upon to explicitly frame our efforts. One additional question can be posed in honoring the place of theology and the synoptic task: What theological question, issue, image, theme, principle, metaphor, passion, need, paradox, and/or dynamic hold a particular work all together? One colleague, Sharon Thornton, helpfully requests that students write their key question visually before them near their computer, desk, or workstation and periodically focus upon it to guide their efforts. For some a recurring image or metaphor can assist in a visually oriented age to maintain one's focus that is suggested by the third commandment of theological research, namely pick a prism. Paulo Freire, a Brazilian public educator and theological educator in his own right, suggested that a truly liberative education involves the posing of questions and problems that this chapter has sought to explore. Clarity with regard to one's questions and answers to those questions, no matter how tentative, contributes greatly to theological research and writing. Theological research and writing are undertaken within diverse theological disciplines that are the topic of chapter 4.

4

Theological Disciplines
and Multidisciplinary Study

THE OPPORTUNITY and gift of theological study at the graduate level enables persons to explore in varying depths theological knowledge and wisdom in the context of life. As noted in
chapter one, theological schools and departments have tended to
be organized around distinct theological disciplines while also
honoring the place of interdisciplinary and more recently multidisciplinary study. It is helpful to understand what comprises a
theological discipline while recognizing that disciplines, similar
to all areas of human life, over time are characterized by continuity and change.

One of my professors in graduate study served as the
faculty chairperson for my doctoral research. He helped me to
better understand the nature and life of an academic and theological discipline as I was being formed to be a participant in
the discipline of religious or Christian education. The fact that
the discipline was called by two names with varying constituen-
cies gathered in two distinct though occasionally overlapping
professional organizations was noteworthy and indicative of the
history.[1] Dwayne Huebner was my professor who insightfully

1. One professional organization was the Association of Professors
and Researchers of Religious Education associated with the Religious
Education Association and the other was the North American Professors
of Christian Education associated with the Professional Association
of Christian Educators. Over the years I have been a member of both

identified ten dimensions of each theological discipline that apply more generally to any academic discipline. I elaborate upon Huebner's insights using over twenty-eight years of personal teaching experience within the theological discipline of Christian education.[2] In relation to each of these dimensions, theological students can gain perspective and orient their research and work to gain knowledge and wisdom for life and ministry. Huebner's ten dimensions are noted with my commentary upon each to help students understand areas they are called to explore and master through their theological work.

1. Community of People—Each discipline is a social structure that is not just intellectual in nature, but gathers people together within a professional community for mutual interaction, learning, and affiliation sustained over time. In relation to the community, participants and those who study with those participants as their professors need to know the key players and various voices or perspectives represented. This knowledge is helpful to discern how those participants may address issues and respond to perennial and current questions and problems in their particular discipline.

2. Expression of Human Imagination—Each discipline relates to the playful and creative handling of questions and problems. Abraham Heschel, as noted in chapter 2 under "wrestle an angel," suggested that religion begins with a question and theology with a problem. In theological research the clear articulation of the question or problem under discussion or study is essential. For those preparing to be clergy, the engagement of pastoral, priestly, or rabbinic

organizations and have served on some of their boards.

2. I draw and elaborate upon Dwayne Huebner's insights from his lecture of November 8, 1978 at Teachers College, Columbia University, New York, New York from his course "Theory of Curriculum Design."

imagination is crucial to nurture as suggested by the study *Educating Clergy* that drew upon the insights of Craig Dykstra. Such imagination is "a distinctive way of seeing and thinking that permeates and shapes clergy practice . . . that integrates knowledge and skill, moral integrity, and religious commitment in the roles, relationships, and responsibilities they will be assuming."[3] For laity, a similar spiritual imagination is required that incarnates one's faith commitments into all areas of personal, professional, and public life.

3. Domain—A discipline points up something it attends to and to certain boundaries of a piece of reality. This implies for theological study an awareness of the limitations of one's work given the situated nature of one's life and the perspective one assumes in viewing the world and the topic under study.

4. Tradition—Every discipline has a history that serves to inform the identity of folk associated with it and the trajectories of the work engaged by participants. For example in the discipline of pastoral psychology, an interest in family systems can be traced back to the insights of Sigmund Freud and Carl G. Jung, who both considered how persons relate to their immediate and human families both consciously and unconsciously.

5. Syntactical Structure—A discipline is a model of inquiry, the way in which things are combined and the forms of analysis, constructive criticism, and creative synthesis. In a language, syntax in general is the way in which words are put together to form phrases, clauses, and sentences. In a theological discipline, syntax refers to how insights cohere and are juxtaposed to form an argument or a perspective embraced. Reading within a theological discipline serves

3. Foster, *Educating Clergy*, 13.

to expose students to the syntactical structures used by scholars and writers.

6. Substance or Conceptual Structure—A theological discipline like other disciplines tends to sustain theoretical frameworks. To study and research within that discipline assumes knowledge of those theorists and theories upon whom others tend to draw. Knowledge of theories requires addressing both the *what* and *why* perennial questions discussed in chapter 3. Students are expected to know what theories and theorists they are drawing upon and why they are important for their own understanding on the topic, question, or issue being studied.

7. Specialized Knowledge—While language varies within disciplines, the proper use of any specialized language is essential. To help clarify the use of language, students are encouraged to define their own terms or to clearly cite the definitions being used to guide the inquiry. Creativity in some areas of study is demonstrated by proposing a new definition or one that critically integrates insights beyond what others suggest.

8. Body of Artifacts, Tools, Literature, Equipment, and Journals—A theological discipline over time has developed approaches, methods, and means by which to study and share the fruits of that study with others. Much is gained by students who gain some competence in reading or gaining familiarity with that body of disciplinary material. At least students can review some of the table of contents for current journals of a particular theological discipline for items of interest. It often impresses one's professor to cite key applicable articles for one's writing topic.

9. Affective Stance—Each discipline tends to embrace an attitude or approach to life, an ethos or tone and quality of life that participants embrace. This dimension suggests the

honoring of heart matters, emotions, and feelings in addition to the head and intellectual matters that are prominent in an academic discipline. This requires writing with one's heart as well as one's head as discussed in chapter 5.

10. Instructive Community—A theological discipline is a community of scholars that instructs neophytes or students. This instruction honors the importance of students gaining their own voice and being one of the conversation partners who can also honor the place of interdisciplinary and multidisciplinary work where significant creativity can be expressed.

The ten dimensions of theological disciplines assist to orient students in their theological research and writing. In addition, the appendices of this work provide samples of specific guidance for research and writing in the four theological disciplines of Old Testament, New Testament, World Christianity, and Practical Theology studies.

INTERDISCIPLINARY
AND MULTIDISCIPLINARY WORK

Theological study provides the opportunity to explore how insights from more than one theological discipline can assist in addressing questions and problems for persons, communities, and societies. Critical and creative theological reflection along with spiritual imagination produces the possibilities of transformative practice in a host of ministry settings and areas of public life. The most creative theological study and scholarship often has an autobiographical connection for students and professors alike. Therefore starting with those questions and problems that emerge from personal, familial, communal, and societal experiences hold the potential of launching inquiry that draws upon various wells or sources found in the theological disciplines. Theological study offers a level of thinking about God recalling the insight of Abraham Heschel who noted that "thinking without roots will bear flowers, but not fruits."[4] Theological study provides the opportunity to think deeply and with wonder about the roots that have nourished faith communities and their participants over the millennia of humankind. The establishment of theological disciplines is a recent historical phenomenon in relation to the history of spiritual traditions of wisdom. Roots of wisdom have informed and formed the perspectives within diverse disciplines. The exploration and tracing of roots enables students to discover the connections by digging deeper. The possibility of integration is weaved by students who draw upon their own experiences in conversation with the wisdom discerned from the roots. To use another metaphor, students' personal stories become conversation partners with both the communal stories and faith stories encountered through theological study. Narrative approaches to theology and ministry explore the connections across the stories with implications for personal and corporate life.

4. Samuel H. Dresner, ed., *I Asked for Wonder: A Spiritual Anthology, Abraham Joshua Heschel* (New York: Crossword, 1995), 83.

5

Writing with Heart and Head

THE FIRST challenge in researching and writing for a particular theological course or assignment is to clarify the distinct
purposes of and guidelines for the task with one's instructor or
advisor. Many faculty colleagues report that students who fail
or struggle with their work did not complete what was actually
assigned, but elected to submit something and in some cases
anything they thought might possibly be acceptable with little
consideration of stated expectations. Meeting one's professor's
expectations may be obvious, but often ignored with disastrous
results. At the graduate level, this is unacceptable if persons expect to master a subject area in a course or qualify to engage
in the depth of study involved in doctoral work. Professors ad-
mittedly are known to be vague on occasion, but this requires
the initiative of students to clarify expectations and to request
assistance from those who will evaluate or grade assignments.
Such clarification is needed well before any research or writing
is launched.

Assuming one has obeyed the five commandments of theological research named in chapter 2 perhaps having been assisted
by one of the three additional approaches identified, tapping into
the heart of writing is essential. The one modern classical work
that has assisted students in discovering the heart of writing is *If
You Want to Write* by Brenda Ueland.[1] The subtitle of this work,

1. Brenda Ueland, *If You Want to Write* (Saint Paul, MN: Graywolf
Press, 1938).

which was added by the publisher, indicates that it is "a book about art, independence and spirit." Ueland plumbs the life-giving sources for creativity and the discovery of one's writing person. She suggests that "writing is talking and thinking on paper."[2] Some students find it very useful to speak their thoughts prior to writing either to other persons or into a recorder. Ueland's motto for writing is "Be bold, be free, be truthful."[3] Ueland enables students to discover the joy of writing in partnership with God's Spirit who enlivens all our spirits for challenging tasks. In the film *Finding Forester*, Sean Connery portrays a renowned author who shares with his young protégé the wisdom: "First you write with your heart, then you rewrite with your head." The title of this chapter mentions first writing with the heart and then the head.

In thinking about theological writing for academic study, the immediate association is the need to follow the required and appointed order within a particular discipline. My statement of the five commandments of theological research via Max Stackhouse honors that order. But a complementary virtue to that of order is the place of ardor in theological research and writing. Ardor honors the place of the heart and the importance of zeal and passion for one's work that can become an expression of one's love for God, neighbor, and all of creation. Theological research and writing can be appreciated as a form of worship. Bishop William Temple defined worship in a liberating and inviting way: "To worship is to quicken the conscience by the holiness of God, to feed the mind with the truth of God, to purge the imagination by the beauty of God, to open the heart to the love of God, to devote the will to the purpose of God."[4] Theological study and research at its best can be worshipful delight for those

2. Ibid., 140.

3. Ibid., x.

4. William Temple, *The Hope of A New World* (London: Student Christian Movement Press, 1941), 30.

called to participate. It is also hard work requiring discipline and diligence, but can result in the following spiritual experience captured in words attributed to Jesus: "Out of the believer's heart shall flow rivers of living water" (John 7:38). Ueland helps to explore the matter of writing with one's heart.

Ueland summarizes the insights of her work on the heart with twelve points that I paraphrase and adapt:

1. Know that you have ability, are original, and have something important to say and write.

2. Know that it is good to work with love and think of liking it when in process. It is interesting and a privilege. What is hard is your anxious vanity and fear of failure.

3. Write freely, recklessly, in first drafts, assuming you have allowed time for multiple drafts.

4. Tackle any subject you want to address within the parameters of your assignment, or negotiate alternatives early on with your instructor.

5. Don't be afraid of writing poorly. Persist and seek out assistance from others.

6. Don't fret or be ashamed of what you have written in the past. Move on to the next task and learn from your experiences.

7. Try to discover your true, honest self in your writing.

8. Think of yourself as an incandescent power, illuminated perhaps and forever talked to by God and God's messengers. Remember how capable and wonderful you are as God's child, created in God's image with gifts and insights to share.

9. If you are never satisfied with what you write, that is a good sign. It means your vision can see far and that it is hard to come up to it.

10. When discouraged, remember what Van Gogh said, "If you hear a voice within you saying: You are no painter, then paint by all means, and that voice will be silenced, but only by working." (Vincent Van Gogh who once was a theological student happens to be my favorite painter.)

11. Don't be afraid of yourself when you write. Don't check yourself.

12. Don't always be appraising yourself, wondering if you are better or worse than others. Because you are like no other being ever created since the beginning of time, you are incomparable.[5]

Ueland provides a way to access the heart of writing with ardor, zeal, passion, enthusiasm, and divine inspiration.

Eviatar Zerubavel in his work *The Clockwork Muse: A Practical Guide to Writing Theses, Dissertations, and Books*, provides a complementary emphasis on order and writing with the head.[6] Whereas Ueland in *If You Want to Write* calls for writing with our heart resulting in inspiration and passion, Zerubavel calls for writing with our head and hands resulting in investment and perspiration. Zerubavel's work does not focus upon theological research and study; nevertheless he provides insights for the writing applicable to theological settings and to works less rigorous than theses, dissertations, and books. His work fosters the exorcising of what I name as the theological research demons that can plague writing at the graduate level. The five chapters of his work with their particular emphases help in the ministry of exorcism to restore a sense of order and to provide guidance for the work or research.

---

5. Euland, *If You Want to Write*, 177–78.

6. Eviatar Zerubavel, *The Clockwork Muse: A Practical Guide to Writing Theses, Dissertations, and Books* (Cambridge, MA: Harvard University Press, 1999).

Chapter 1 of *The Clockwork Muse* emphasizes the need for planning and the use of a regular schedule that results in slow and steady work in one's research and writing. Upon receiving an assignment or in undertaking a major writing effort, planning serves to realistically set parameters for one's time and energy working backwards from one's due date allowing for the various contingencies of life beyond theological study.

Chapter 2 of Zerubavel's work, "The Writing Schedule," explores regularity and organization. It calls for devoting sufficient time along with knowing when to stop. Knowing when to stop is often a challenge with the research phase of theological work prior to writing. There is always a new book or article to consider and the use of the word "no" is timely to restrict what can be an unending process and escalating frustrations due to time pressures. Discipline and flexibility allow for avoiding conflicts with other commitments. Helpful advice is to decide when and how often you plan to write and plan to take a walk. Walking often provides the creative space to use one's body and loosen thoughts that may be jumbled and confused. Walking can also occasion a time to pray for wisdom (James 1:5).

Chapter 3, "A Mountain with Stairs," provides the suggestion to chunk down one's work and to keep going with the writing even while awaiting possible responses from others who have agreed to review or comment on your work. I have found that the response of others always serves to improve my writing. What may be clear and logical to me may make little sense to first time readers, even those who may know me well. This should not be discouraging with the multiple challenges of communication and the need to provide adequate explanation for others who are willing to decipher our writing.

Chapter 4, "The Project Timetable," suggests the need to take time off occasionally. Such advice assumes that writing has not been left for the last minute with little soak time for the topic and ideas explored in research. This chapter points up that Sabbath is important along with a focus on the work to be accomplished.

Zerubavel's fifth and final chapter, "The Mechanics of Progress," encourages his readers to write freely and rapidly, keep moving along, back up and print out drafts regularly, set deadlines, write down ideas as soon as you have them, develop a discipline, and keep on keeping on. Such advice values persistence that is an echo of the fifth commandment of theological research from chapter 2 of this work, namely "Read, Formulate (or write), Talk, Read, and Reformulate (or rewrite)." Both sources honor a process and a discipline calling for a sustained commitment over time. Diligence makes a difference and is honored with improved skills and results provided we do not grow weary in our well doing. Galatians 6:9 suggests such: "So let us not grow weary in doing what is right, for we will reap at harvest time, if we do not give up."

In a course that I teach on theological research I first have students read Ueland's work *If You Want to Write*. I want them to start with their heart in order to tap into the passion, interest, and motivation to sustain their research and writing. Second I ask them to read Zerubavel's work *The Clockwork Muse* to engage their heads. In revisiting their heartfelt insights, their heady review and analysis can foster communication with others who will read their work. This process is also valuable in preparing work for publication with readers that include colleagues, publishers, editors, and anyone else who may graciously agree to read your work. The writing first with the heart to tap into ardor is complemented with then writing with the head in hopes of providing some intelligible order to one's insights resulting in a creative and critical work. One of the goals of theological education as identified in chapter 1 is to foster creative and critical theological reflection that finds expression in writing, speaking, and ministering in the world. In the process of that intellectual work we realize the need for sources of wisdom beyond ourselves. Chapter 6 considers spiritual resources beyond our personal capacities.

6

A Spiritual Practice

THE OPPORTUNITY to study, research, and write in theological education can be seen as an invitation to embrace a spiritual practice that has origins with the creation of humankind. Spiritual practices assume a connection with particular religious traditions and communities that for me center upon the Christian heritage. Genesis 1:2 describes the Spirit of God hovering over the waters and being present when humans are called into being as God said, "Let us make humankind in our image, according to our likeness" (Gen. 1:26). John's gospel provides further theological reflection:

> In the beginning was the Word, and the Word was with God, and the Word was God. He was in the beginning with God. All things came into being through him, and without him not one thing came into being. What has come into being in him was life, and the life was the light of all people (John 1:1–4).

The Word as God's fullest expression later to appear in human form as Jesus the Christ, is described by the gospel writer as present and party to the coming into being of all things, including persons with their capacity for reflection on life itself. Theological education offers an opportunity to reflect upon God, creation, and life in communion with others. Those others include the persons of God, Jesus Christ, and the Spirit named collectively in Christian theology as the Trinity. Persons created in God's image along with their bodies have spirits that are called to be in communion with the Holy Spirit described as the Spirit of Truth (John 15:26) who will guide Jesus' disciples into all truth (John 16:13). Theological education is an enterprise that strives to discern truth and meaning in the world. In that effort those who seek to learn must be open to a relationship with the Holy Spirit in order to discern her promptings and workings.

Other spiritual traditions beyond the Christian heritage can be explored in addressing the religious plurality of the third millennium, but fruitful dialogue requires an initial embrace of one's particular identity while engaging a wider encounter.[1] Two challenges for theological students persist in a time of religious pluralism. The first challenge is to explore and affirm one's own religious and spiritual identity and the second is to engage a wider encounter with neighbors from diverse religious traditions. The hope in such an encounter is to not only embrace with clarity what one brings to a common table, but to be open to deeper appreciation of what other traditions offer, avoiding divisive conflicts that have marred the history of interfaith exchange and collision. The search for truth in theological education avoids an arrogance of assuming one's version of the truth is the final word and refusing to acknowledge the limitations of a particular perspective. Such an open-ended stance of the mind does not exclude a whole-hearted embrace of one's community's faith personally appropriated and celebrated publicly. The derision and hatred of those who differ theologically must confront the reality that God reserves the right to use and bless those who disagree with me theologically. Thank God for this reality that calls for academic and theological humility in receiving revela-

---

1. For a description of my wider encounter with diverse religious traditions see Robert W. Pazmiño, *By What Authority Do We Teach? Sources for Empowering Christian Educators* (Eugene, OR: Wipf and Stock, 2002), 119–46. This chapter is entitled "Authority of Truth in an Age of Pluralism" and notes what I learned from this wider dialogue.

tion and acknowledging mystery in religious faith and reflection upon that faith in theological education.

My perspective is tempered through the observation of religious and theological fundamentalism on both the left and right of theological positions. I also maintain a bias to consider the both/and option on theological questions and recognize the place of paradox in life and faith. The Apostle Paul reflecting upon the imitation of Christ's example suggested the following: "Do nothing from selfish ambition or conceit, but in humility regard others as better than yourselves. Let each of you look not to your own interests, but to the interests of others" (Phil 2:3–4). I think this insight can apply to learning in theological education while encountering differences across a host of variables in the third millennium. I think it is important to be convinced of one's own position theologically through study, but to be gracious in understanding how others come to different conclusions. The actual articulation of how I differ from others can communicate as much as the content of my positions. In other words, theological education calls for openness to new learnings offered by God's Spirit to those who have ears to hear, inquiring minds to explore, and pliable hearts to engage truth with love. These are high ideals for theological education, but ones that assume the character formation of spirits as well as minds.

SPIRITUAL PRACTICES THAT SUSTAIN STUDY

Karl Barth, famed Swiss theologian shared a noteworthy observation: "Theological work can be done only in the indissoluble unity of prayer and study. Prayer without study would be empty. Study without prayer would be blind."[2] Prayer is essential before, during, and after theological study in keeping with one of my favorite Bible memory verses of 1 Thessalonians 5:17 from Sunday

2. Karl Barth, *Evangelical Theology: An Introduction.* Trans. Grover Foley (Garden City, NY: Doubleday & Co., 1964), 151.

School instruction, "Pray without ceasing." Along with the prior verse of 1 Thessalonians 5:16, "Rejoice always," theological studies have pithy scriptural wisdom to consider. Even when assignments in theological school are due the book of James provides the additional practical advice and promise: "If any of you is lacking in wisdom, ask God, who gives generously and ungrudgingly, and it will be given you" (Jas 1:5). Prayer provides the occasion to ask God for such wisdom provided it is accompanied with diligent study.

An ecumenical study of spiritual formation conducted by the Programme on Theological Education of the World Council of Churches in 1987 identified seven factors as being essential for Christian spiritual formation related to theological study. Students can consider these seven over the long haul of their study and not just during the crunch times of paper writing

1. "Spiritual formation is always lived and sought in community."

A seminary "community should be characterized by an atmosphere of personal trust, absence of unhealthy competition and stress, responsible freedom and participation, openness and readiness to share each other's problems and weaknesses."[3] This ideal of community is a challenge for practice because it requires the commitment of individuals in a seminary setting.

2. "Engagement in scholarly study of scriptures and theology must be seen as integral to the processes of spiritual formation."

"Scholarship opens new horizons. . . . Intellectual excellence and spiritual depth are not opposed to each other, but they support

---

3. *Spiritual Formation in Theological Education: An Invitation to Participate* (Geneva: Programme on Theological Education, World Council of Churches, 1987), 17.

each other."[4] The two dangers of anti-intellectualism and academic arrogance need to be avoided in theological study.

3. "Times for silence and retreat, private and corporate, often provide helpful means of sustaining Christian spirituality."[5]

To this I would add the place of corporate service learning as a regularly scheduled event for theological students and faculty alike beyond field education experiences.

4. "Spiritual formation should always be related to a local community of believers."[6]

A time of huddling with theological students and faculty needs the complementary mixing with believers from across the age span and intergenerational worship, learning, and service. Such is primarily experienced in local congregations, but also possible in other ministry settings beyond the walls of theological schools.

5. "Spiritual growth is fostered by direct exposure to the harsh realities of this life and encounter with the problems of our world."[7]

Coming apart for theological study and reflection is for the purpose of engaging the world with spiritual resources offered with open hands, hearts, and minds.

6. "Experiencing various liturgical and worshipping traditions is a means of enrichment in spiritual formation, which will encourage growth towards a spirituality that is inclusive of the diversity of the spiritual wealth of the whole people of God."[8]

4. Ibid., 17–18.
5. Ibid., 18.
6. Ibid.
7. Ibid.
8. Ibid.

Each believer has preferred spiritual dispositions that are stretched and deepened in fellowship with others from diverse spiritual traditions.

7. "Opportunities for ecumenical and cross-cultural exchange provide chances for realizing that a given type of spirituality is not universal, and that spirituality is not the property of Christians alone."[9]

The identity of one's particular spirituality is complemented by openness to one's neighbors in an increasingly religious and spiritual plurality within local communities.

Beyond the insights noted from this ecumenical study of spiritual formation, theological educators have explored specific faith practices essential to spiritual formation. In the work *The God Bearing Life*, Kenda Creasy Dean and Ron Foster creatively identify six families of Christian practices that are noteworthy not only for youth, but adults as well. They are creatively named and include worship–praise making, communion–bread breaking, compassion–pain taking, teaching/nurture–wave making, witness–claim staking, and dehabituation–rhythm breaking.[10] Theological education provides opportunities to explore these spiritual practices biblically, theologically, historically, ethically, and practically while developing skills in their transformative expression in ministry today and in the future. Greater attention currently is being given to the intentional effort of teaching persons these practices within Protestant settings learning from what has been more explicit in both Catholic and Orthodox theological schools.

9. Ibid.

10. Kenda Creasy Dean and Ron Foster, *The God Bearing Life: The Art of Soul Tending for Youth Ministry* (Nashville: Upper Room Books, 1998), 105–22.

7

Practical Advice

THEOLOGICAL EDUCATION while focusing on theology is itself a form of education. Education in general can be defined as a process that shares content with persons in the context of their community and society. In the case of theological education that content is the study of *theos* or God. Education in general attends to the three elements of content, persons, and context that the prior six chapters have explored for the particular case of theological education. But as my definition for education suggests, theological education is also a process that can assist persons to navigate through their experiences in a theological school. What practical advice can help guide the process of theological education?

Theological students can first note that the content of theological education engages their head, heart, and hands. The head is engaged through the academic and intellectual challenge of exploring questions and problems while studying God and life in God's creation. The heart is engaged in first writing with one's heart as discussed in chapter 5 and embracing spiritual practices as noted in chapter 6. The hands are engaged in doing the reading, research, and writing noted throughout this guide. The hands are also engaged by living in community with others in a theological school and through service both within and beyond the setting of a theological community in various ministry settings. This final chapter provides some practical advice for one's hands in doing theological research. While engaging their hands, theological students are nurturing their hearts and heads in what hopefully is a holistic experience that enables them to theologically reflect, spiritually imagine, and transformatively practice their faith. I identify practical suggestions to facilitate the process of theological education for all those called to this joyful venture.

START EARLY

To allow for a process rather than a last minute crunch it is crucial to allot sufficient time for the research phases of theological inquiry prior to actual writing. In order to write with both heart and head, time is also crucial between those two phases of expressing one's thoughts in a coherent and intelligible fashion in graduate study. If one's professor is to be consulted and peers provided an opportunity to read one's work for comments and suggestions, time must be factored into one's plans. All this suggests the need to start early and perhaps begin planning as soon as one's assignments for a semester or term are given. As noted earlier working back from the due date of an assignment can assist in outlining reasonable benchmarks to guide efforts and enable a successful completion of work.

ASK FOR HELP

If theological education is to foster a communal experience where "iron sharpens iron," students are to be open to ask for help from their instructors and peers. Christian faith affirms a corporate identity as children of God, the body of Christ, and the temple of the Holy Spirit. In the context of a theological school, one expression of that spiritual reality is fostered when students request and receive support for their theological research. We cannot do it alone in life and in the life of theological study seeking out the help and support of others besides God enables us to learn from others in community. In the United States this poses a challenge for dominant cultural patterns of independence and destructive personalism. Theological study is an invitation to explore collaborative and cooperative patterns of living and working together.

SHARE YOUR WORK

What is implicit in my last suggestion, but needs further emphasis is the need to share one's work or writing at various stages. This supports the insights of Brenda Ueland in chapter 5 who encourages us to write with all of our hearts. That effort is complemented by taking the risks of sharing our work with others for their honest and hopefully not too brutal responses. Our writing requires the eyes and thoughts of others to improve and to effectively communicate beyond our personal sphere. Some instructors are willing to respond to outlines and initial drafts for their comments provided my first suggestion of starting early is followed. At least requesting a meeting to discuss the plans for one's work provides a wonderful occasion to gain perspective, learn of additional resources, and make early corrections in clarifying an assignment.

LET GO WITH PRAYER

Some select theological students can spend inordinate time in researching while avoiding the actual writing of their findings. At appointed times in one's schedule, it is essential to begin writing. Replicating a timed test can assist those who procrastinate rather than launch the writing process. To facilitate the launch into writing, it can help to commit the writing process to God in prayer and let go of the fascination of always doing more research. This side of heaven, no writing effort is complete in the sense of discovering and expressing the final definitive word on any subject. Letting go and committing one's work in prayer can move the process forward in a creative way. Letting go can create space for the fermentation and connection of ideas that engages the right side of the brain. Committing one's work to God in prayer allows space for the creative Holy Spirit to direct our human spirit and imagination.

LEARN FROM FEEDBACK

Once one's work is completed and submitted, the opportunity to openly receive affirmation and constructive criticism exists. The process of theological education requires edification where persons of faith are being built up together in fulfilling God's calling in the world. Instructors are those who have traveled ahead of us along life's journey (at least in their theological discipline) and beyond the concern for grades is the opportunity to learn in a theological school. Some learning or discipline can be viewed as harsh as Hebrews 12:11 suggests: "Now, discipline always seems painful rather than pleasant at the time, but later it yields the peaceful fruit of righteousness to those who have been trained by it." The hope is for positive learning experiences in theological school, yet I have probably learned the most from my failures over my life time and in my theological education.

CONCLUSION

This simple practical advice may be helpful in honoring the process intended for theological study. Others' works provide more detailed specifics that vary with the theological discipline in which one is working. These works are noted both in the Annotated Bibliography and Appendices of this book.

Conclusion

THIS GUIDE has shared basics about conducting research for those called to theological study. The venture of theological education is an essential task to sustain the world as God's creation in the hearts and minds of each generation. The joy of this venture is the potential it holds as a form of worship that brings glory to God. I have been privileged to engage in this venture as my life's calling and highly commend it to all who see it as an opportunity to love God with all of our heart, soul, mind, and strength.

The Appendices of this work provide additional assistance for research and writing with sample guides for particular theological disciplines.

Annotated Bibliography

Ammerman, Nancy, Jackson W. Carroll, Carl S. Dudley, and William McKinney, eds. *Studying Congregations: A New Handbook*. Nashville: Abingdon Press, 1998. An essential work for those pursuing doctoral study that focuses on life in congregations.

Barber, Cyril, and Robert M. Krauss, Jr. *An Introduction to Theological Research: A Guide for College and Seminary Students*. 2d ed. Lanham, MD: University Press of America, 2000. A guide more for college work with assignments to explore research tools. A wealth of reference works is noted and helps with online searching.

Booth, Wayne C., Gregory G. Colomb, and Joseph M. Williams. *The Craft of Research*. 2d ed. Chicago: University of Chicago Press, 2003. An excellent introduction to research in general that provides key steps to clarify one's research topic.

Brown, Michael Joseph. *What They Don't Tell You: A Survivor's Guide to Biblical Studies*. Louisville: Westminster John Knox, 2000. This work explores biblical studies in depth. Twenty-eight rules of thumb to observe in biblical exegesis are explored.

Cetuk, Virginia Samuel. *What to Expect in Seminary: Theological Education as Spiritual Formation*. Nashville: Abingdon Press, 1998. This work uses the lens of spiritual formation and ministry to explore seminary education. The inclusion of exercises enables students to use this work as a workbook for issues confronted in the process.

Core, Deborah. *The Seminary Student Writes*. St. Louis: Chalice Press, 2000. Wisdom and practical guidance from a professor of English and fellow seminary student is shared to navigate the writing process and expectations in theological education.

Kepple, Robert J., and John R. Muether. *Reference Works for Theological Rresearch: An Annotated Selective Bibliographic Guide*. 3d ed.

Lanham, MD: University Press of America, 1992. An extensive listing of resources arranged by theological discipline.

Miller, Donald E., and Barry Jay Seltser. *Writing and Research in Religious Studies*. Englewood Cliffs, NJ: Prentice Hall, 1992. Offers a wealth of practical advice and specific instructions for step-by-step procedures to cover the details of religious research and writing.

Myers, William. *Research in Ministry: A Primer for the Doctor of Ministry Program*. 3d ed. Chicago: Exploration Press, 2000. For those in a DMin program this provides introduction to use of a case study method to guide research. A useful annotated bibliography is included.

Turabian, Kate L. *A Manual for Writers of Term Papers, Thesis, and Dissertations*. 6th ed. Chicago: University of Chicago Press, 1996. An indispensable guide for the form and format of writing and referencing works following the *Chicago Manual of Style*.

Ueland, Brenda. *If You Want To Write: A Book about Art, Independence and Spirit*. Saint Paul: Graywolf Press, 1987. A classic work that explores the heart of writing with ardor, passion, and vision. Ueland can serve as a midwife for writers.

Vyhmeister, Nancy Jean. *Your Indispensable Guide to Writing Quality Research Papers for Students of Religion and Theology*. Grand Rapids: Zondervan, 2001. This work provides a detailed approach to the "nuts and bolts" of theological writing in depth.

Westerhoff, John H. *Spiritual Life: The Foundation for Preaching and Teaching*. Louisville: Westminster John Knox, 1994. This work explores spiritual life as a love affair with God and distinct schools of spirituality. A must read for seminarians.

Zerubavel, Eviatar. *The Clockwork Muse: A Practical Guide to Writing Theses, Dissertations, and Books*. Cambridge: Harvard University Press, 1999. Suggests an order for steady writing and how best to get organized with larger writing projects.

Appendix A

A Brief Guide to New Testament Exegesis

Professor Sze-kar Wan

A N EXEGESIS paper is a coherent essay on the interpretation of a biblical passage. "Interpretation" is a slippery term, but here it refers to the historical meaning of a passage as intended by the author. In other words, exegesis tries to answer the question, "What does the author mean?" by taking into account the author's historical circumstance, purpose, language, style, etc.

> Advice: It is well known that understanding a work in its entirety is based on understanding the parts that make up the whole, and that the interpretation of individual passages is by necessity related to the interpretation of the whole work. This hermeneutical circle could easily become a vicious cycle if the interpreter does not take seriously the starting point: namely, the passage at hand. Beginners are often tempted to deduce the meaning of a passage from the supposed stable meaning of the whole work. Resist this temptation. The goal of exegesis is to reconstruct the meaning of individual passages inductively; then and only then does one have the necessary building blocks for the whole edifice.

An exegesis paper is a *coherent* essay, which, like any other cogently written essay, includes, at the very least, an effective introduction, carefully delineated arguments, and a persuasive conclusion. It is not just a collection of disjointed notes or desultory comments, even though it is often based on such a collection; notes and comments are constitutive elements to a persuasive argument but not the argument itself. Nor is an exegesis paper a personal reflection *or* a sermon, even though a personal reflection or sermon can benefit from sound exegesis.

A good exegesis paper is based on two principles: Sound Methodology and Clear Presentation.

SOUND METHODOLOGY

Sound methodology in biblical exegesis means following these steps:

1. Establishing the Text—There are thousands of manuscripts on the Bible and multiple readings on any given verse—hence the need for textual criticism. The exegete must decide which variant has the highest probability of being the original reading. If you read Greek, use the apparatus in your Greek Bible and consult Metzger's Textual Commentary on the NT for the merits of the variants. (See Bibliographical Aids below.) If you do not read Greek, use different translations to discover if there are textual issues in your passage.

2. Coming up with a Provisional Translation—Any translation is interpretation of a sort; a provisional translation helps jump-start your thought process and give you a foundation for your investigation. As you understand the text better, you will change the translation accordingly. Translate the Greek text if you know Greek; otherwise, use multiple translations to help you translate the passage.

3. Investigating the Historical Context—What do you know about the immediate occasion of the work and of the passage at hand? What possible connection, if any, might there be between your passage and external civil and political

events? Good commentaries that pay attention to such historical details are indispensable in this regard, but do not let commentaries influence your exegetical decisions prematurely. (However, see no. 8 below.)

4. Investigating the Literary Context and Structure—The passage is a part of a larger literary unit; determine its relation to the larger context within the work. Read the whole book. Then carefully analyze the preceding and ensuing contexts of said passage. Analyze, finally, the passage itself and delineate its argumentative or narrative structure.

5. Determining the Traditional Character of your Passage—If your passage is traditional (i.e., if it comes from a source), determine whether and to what extent the author has modified the meaning of the original. In the letters, determine whether the author is making use of a preexisting hymn, formula, Septuagint (LXX), saying of Jesus, etc. When working with the synoptic Gospels, be sure to compare all relevant parallel passages. Whenever you encounter more than one layer of tradition, at all times be clear about which layer you have in mind when attributing meaning. Do not, for example, confuse the views of the historical Jesus with the theology of Matthew or Paul's views with those of his quoted material.

6. Studying Key Terms in the Passage—Since an author might have used terms and expressions that meant something entirely different from their modern equivalents, it is imperative that you consult lexicons, dictionaries, concordances to reconstruct the historical meaning of a term or expression. These tools place key words and concepts in their historical settings and help you evaluate how they were used. Even if you have no Greek, it is still possible to use these important tools with great profit. (See Bibliographic Aids below.)

7. Reconstructing the Original Meaning—After you have examined all the nuts and bolts, you are ready to reassemble the parts into a unified whole. What is the meaning of your passage *as intended by the historical author?* Does the evidence point to a cogent message? A useful technique at this stage of the game is to write a provisional draft of your paper.

Advice: Do this step as soon as possible, even if you feel you are not ready. In so doing, you might discover you need to do additional research or recheck your text or sources. This is an intermediate check, a progress report to yourself.

8. Consulting Commentaries—After you have done the groundwork, see what others have done with your passage. Learned commentators seldom agree with each other on all points, but you are now equipped to evaluate whether and to what extent you agree with one commentator against another. Choose four to six commentators for this purpose but do not over-research; you may find it difficult to integrate too much material in the allotted time. Consult also scholarly articles in learned journals. (See Bibliographical Aids below.)

Advice: Do not rely exclusively on one-volume commentaries (even one as good as *The New Jerome Bible Commentary*) or such popular series as *The Interpreter's Bible;* these are intended as reading guides, not exegetical works.

9. Coming up with a Final Translation—The confidence with which you can defend your translation is often a fair indicator of how well you understand the passage.

The sequence of your actual research may vary slightly from the above, but it is important that you do not skip any step.

CLEAR PRESENTATION

The order of discovery is not necessarily the order of presentation. A clearly presented paper might assume the following format

1. Introduction—Define what the exegetical issues are, state your hypothesis clearly and succinctly in one or two paragraphs, and tell your readers how you intend to test your hypothesis. The goal of an introduction is to draw a clear, accurate road map to guide your readers. You have important things to say; make sure your readers are on board when you set out.

Advice: Do not restate historical information one could easily find in a standard textbook. For example, do not begin the paper with "Corinth was a city in Greece . . . " or "Paul was born in Tarsus . . . " or "Galatians is a letter Paul wrote to the churches in Galatia . . . ," etc. Your readers are your peers who in all likelihood already have such information. They are far more interested in the fruits of your research and judgment.

2. Arguments and Evidence—The main body of your paper, this section might include your structural analysis of the passage, your word studies, your research, or any evidence or deduction that might lend support to your exegetical decisions.

Advice: You might be tempted simply to enumerate your impressive research point by point. Remember, though your readers are intelligent, they did not accompany you when you made your discoveries. You must, therefore, construct bridges connecting your raw arguments and reiterate directions to your destination. Aim persistently at leading your readers to draw the same conclusion you have drawn for yourself.

3. Conclusion—After the presentation of your evidence, take your readers to your conclusion and impress them with

what a worthwhile journey it has been. If your arguments are complex, add a brief summary before drawing your conclusions. Always try to go beyond mere summarization, however.

Advice: You could here indicate how your closely argued thesis might be useful for such issues as spiritual growth, sermon preparation, theological reflections, etc. This is your opportunity to reintroduce your thoughts and your very self into the larger personal or ministerial context.

4. Final Translation of the Passage—Include, if you wish, a readable translation that represents the fruit of your investigation. Present it as an appendix.

This outline is meant to be suggestive and is by no means binding. Clarity ought not spell the end of creativity.

BIBLIOGRAPHICAL AIDS

Four small but useful books may help you understand further the theory and practice of New Testament exegesis:

Fee, Gordon. *New Testament Exegesis.* Rev. ed. Leominster: Gracewing; Louisville: Westminster/John Knox Press, 1993. A very practical and methodical guide; highly recommended.

Harrington, Daniel J. *Interpreting the New Testament: A Practical Guide.* Wilmington: Glazier, 1979. Less methodical than Fee but contains fuller discussions of various exegetical theories like form criticism.

Harrington, Daniel J. *The New Testament: A Bibliography.* Wilmington: Glazier, 1985. More up to date than Scholer below.

Scholer, David M. *A Basic Bibliographic Guide for New Testament Exegesis.* 2d ed. Grand Rapids: Eerdmans, 1973.

A somewhat dated now but still useful guide to tools for New Testament exegesis; compare with Harrington's *Bibliography*.

Ultimately, though these guides may point you in the right direction, there is no substitute for getting your exegetical finger nails dirty and "doing exegesis" yourself.

Texts and Text Criticism

Text criticism is the method of establishing the original reading of the text from the hundreds of New Testament manuscripts. The United Bible Societies pooled together important scholars in the field and produced:

The Greek New Testament. 4th ed. United Bible Societies, 1993.

To evaluate the text-critical decisions made by the UBS editorial committee members, you might want to consult the companion volume:

Metzger, Bruce M. *A Textual Commentary on the New Testament*. London/New York: United Bible Societies, 1971. Read the Introduction for a brief discussion of the various manuscript types and have a taste of text criticism.

Interlinear Bible, Analytical Lexicons, and Concordances

An *interlinear Bible* prints a word-for-word literal English translation between the Greek lines (hence the name). It helps non-Greek readers to locate Greek words through the English. If you know Greek, however, *do not* use this tool; it can become a crutch that hampers your ability to handle the Greek text in the long run. Use the following interlinear Bible, if you must, which is based on the NRSV:

Brown, Robert K., and Philip W. Comfort, trans., J. D. Douglas, ed. *The New Greek-English Interlinear New Testament*. Wheaton, IL: Tyndale, 1990.

Once you locate the Greek word in your passage, use an *analytical lexicon* to look up the "lexical form." Greek is an inflectional language, meaning the word as it appears in your text might look significantly different in the dictionaries and concordances, entries in which are all keyed by the lexical form. The following analytical lexicon is published in an attractive format:

Mounce, William D. *The Analytical Lexicon to the Greek New Testament*. Grand Rapids: Zondervan, 1993.

A *New Testament concordance* lists all occurrences of a word in the New Testament in canonical order. Examine all these references to find out how the word is used by your author elsewhere in the New Testament as well as by other early Christian authors. Take a look at the following:

Wigram, George V., and Ralph D. Winter, eds. *The Word Study Concordance*. Pasadena: William Carey Library, 1972. Based on English, which makes it less useful if you are working with the Greek text.

Aland, K. *et alii. Vollständige Konkordanz zum griechischen Neuen Testament*. Berlin/New York: de Gruyter, 1975–. A complete concordance, as the title indicates, based on the Greek text.

Lexicons

A *lexicon* is a full-fledged Greek-English dictionary that also discusses nuances of a word in different passages as well as includes very useful references to ancient Christian and non-Christian writers. The following are both highly trustworthy:

Danker, Frederick W., ed. *A Greek-English Lexicon of the New Testament and Other Early Christian Literature*. 3d ed.

Chicago: University of Chicago Press, 2000. A thoroughly revised (by Danker) version of the longstanding standard lexicon in New Testament studies by Walter Bauer, W. Arndt, F. W. Gingrich, and F. W. Danker; with a new stress on discussion of words in essay (rather than tabular) form. Indispensable for serious students of the New Testament.

Liddell, Henry George, and Robert Scott. *A Greek-English Lexicon*. 2 vols. Oxford: Clarendon Press, 1925. Standard Greek-English lexicon for *all* Greek literature, with copious references to Greek authors of all ages from Homer to Church Fathers; should be used in conjunction with Danker for New Testament studies.

Theological Dictionaries

For a full discussion of the background of a word, its historical development in Classical and Hellenistic Greek, Biblical and Rabbinic Hebrew, as well as LXX and New Testament usages, its theological import in the literature, its synonyms, etc., consult a *theological dictionary*. These dictionaries give not only definitions of a word but also its philosophical and theological connotations. While enormously learned, these works represent scholarly judgments by authors who are subject to the usual prejudices and biases. To make use of such prodigious scholarship, the exegete must therefore be willing to evaluate these works with a healthy sense of suspicion. The following are highly recommended:

Balz, Horst, and Gerhard Schneider, eds. *Exegetical Dictionary of the New Testament*. 3 vols. ET. Grand Rapids: Eerdmans, Ger., 1978–80. A cross between a lexicon and a theological dictionary, with more up-to-date bibliography than some of the classical works like Kittel-Friedrich. Intended for students whose Greek is weak or nonexistent. It is keyed to individual words in Greek.

Brown, Colin, ed. *New International Dictionary of NT Theology*. 4 vols. Grand Rapids: Zondervan, 1975–86. A so-called "concept-lexicon" (*Begriffswörterbuch*) keyed to groups of synonyms in English rather than individual words in Greek. Greek and scriptural indexes are included in vol. 4.

Kittel, Gerhard, and Gerhard Friedrich, eds. *Theological Dictionary of the New Testament*. ET. 10 vols. Grand Rapids: Eerdmans, Ger., 1933–78. The granddaddy of them all; keyed to individual word-stems in Greek; very learned and exhaustive; provides good background material in greater detail than you will ever need; enormously useful if you stay with it. Earlier volumes were published before WWII. Volume 10 includes useful indexes. There is an abbreviated one-volume work under the same title.

Looking up Technical Terms

For newcomers to biblical exegesis, the plethora of technical terms might seem bewildering and intimidating. Look these terms up in:

Soulen, Richard. Handbook of Biblical Criticism. Atlanta: John Knox, 1976. Short definitions arranged in alphabetical order.

For more detailed information, you should consult relevant articles in these more comprehensive dictionaries:

The HarperCollins Dictionary of Religion. 15 vols. San Francisco: HarperSanFrancisco, 1995. Comprehensive and up-to-date.

Interpreter's Dictionary of the Bible. 4 vols. New York & Nashville: Abingdon, 1962; and *Interpreter's Dictionary of the Bible Supplementary Volume*. Nashville: Abingdon, 1976. Rather dated by now but still contains valuable information.

Dictionary of Jesus and the Gospels. Downers Grove: InterVarsity Press, 1992. Specialized dictionary on Gospel studies by English and North American scholars; representative of the best of evangelical scholarship.

Dictionary of Paul and his Letters. Downers Grove: InterVarsity Press, 1993. A companion volume on Pauline studies by a similar group of scholars as above.

Finding Scholarly Articles on your Passage

New Testament Abstracts are published three times a year indexing and abstracting all articles in New Testament studies. This is especially useful for works that are written in an inaccessible language, since every reference includes a short abstract in English. All the articles are listed in canonical order; there is also a comprehensive Scripture-index included at end of each year (no. 3 of each volume).

The Religious Studies Index includes all categories of religious studies and does not abstract the articles. It is less useful to New Testament exegetes, but it is available on a CD-ROM and is easier to use.

Appendix B

Exegesis of the Old Testament

PROFESSOR GREGORY MOBLEY

"EXEGESIS" OFTEN seems like a vaguely threatening word. Do not have anxieties about the word, which may seem like part of the special code Bible professors use. I will use the word but it carries no special weight for me.

Note what Leander Keck says:

> There is nothing mysterious about "exegesis." It is simply the Greek word . . . which means "bringing out"—hence, bringing out the meaning (NIB 1:2).

In other words, your task is to carefully read and orderly describe what happens in a biblical text in order to answer the question best posed by Hal David (with music by Burt Bacharach): "What's it all about, Alfie?"

In the study of the Old Testament we will sample and read about various methods of doing exegesis—this criticism and that criticism—and all of them have their time and place. In the end, the Bible is diverse and some methods are better for one passage than another. Bible interpreters are certainly diverse and, whether because of nature or nurture, certain methods have greater or lesser appeal to them. Furthermore, Bible audiences are diverse and a responsible interpreter must also consider what method is most useful for her or his audience.

But since this is an introductory course, I am going to boss you around.

Here's what you should do with your passage. I want you to perform a watered-down version of Phyllis Trible's *Rhetorical Criticism* on the text. Do not be scared off by the title. I mention it only to impress you.

Whether we call it rhetorical criticism or not, this kind of analysis, I contend, is the bread and butter of effective biblical interpretation. You cannot go wrong if you follow these steps.

Perhaps its best practitioner is Trible, who taught at Andover Newton Theological School early in her career. To see how she does it, consult:

"The Book of Jonah," *NIB* vol. 7;

God and Rhetoric of Sexuality, Overtures to Biblical Theology (Philadelphia: Fortress, 1978);

Texts of Terror: Literary-Feminist Readings of Biblical Narratives, Overtures to Biblical Theology (Philadelphia: Fortress, 1984);

Rhetorical Criticism: Context, Method, and the Book of Jonah, Guides to Biblical Scholarship (Minneapolis: Fortress, 1994).

Here are some guidelines, modified from Trible (*Rhetorical Criticism*, 101–6).

1. "Begin with the text."

> Read it again and again. . . . Jot down ideas that come your way. Some you may never use, but they all help to get the process started.

2. "Read various scholarly works on the text and take notes." At this point, you must be careful from the beginning to note ideas and actual words that you have borrowed from others so that, if you end up using them, you can give credit where credit is due. These ideas and words are the intellectual children of scholars. If you use them as your own, without attribution, you have committed plagiarism, which is Latin for "kidnapping."

3. "Beginning and ending."

This is the fundamental task, figuring out where your unit begins and ends.

> Though some boundaries are given (e.g., a book, psalm, or proverb), others require establishing (e.g., a story or poem within a larger whole). To determine limits, use the criterion of form and content. Make certain the two elements cohere. On a difficult text several tries may be necessary before beginning and ending fall into place. Even critics may disagree.

In other words, find a chunk of Scripture that, at some level, can stand on its own.

This is tricky. On one level, the entire Christian Bible from Genesis to Revelation is a unit, beginning with a garden paradise and ending with an urban paradise (is the divine plan of the ages to get people to move from the country to the city?). The primary history is a unit, from Genesis to Kings, which could be read as a single story from primeval community in Eden (Gen 1–2) followed by exile (Gen 3), to creation of the Israelite covenant community in the Promised Land (Gen 11 forward) followed by exile (in Babylon, at the end of 2 Kgs). The Pentateuch can be read as a unit, again from creation to the portrait of Moses's heroic, Lincolnesque loneliness on Mount Nebo at the end of Deuteronomy. The Deuteronomistic history, from Joshua to Kings, is a unit, from entrance into the land to exit from the land. Most of the individual books of the Bible are, at some level, self-contained units (though there are places, such as between 1 and 2 Sam and between 1 and 2 Kgs where the breaks are artificial). Etc.

For practical purposes, whether in analysis or preaching or teaching or personal devotions, it is wise to seek smaller, more digestible units.

What I want to train you to do is to make your cuts at seams that actually exist in the texture of the biblical material so that you do not rip the fabric.

You may choose a given episode in a larger story, such as with Genesis 27, Jacob's stealing of Esau's firstborn blessing, which is one section of the larger saga of Jacob (which is itself a section of the larger ancestral history, which is itself a part of Genesis, which is . . .). On other occasions you may focus on one scene of an episode, or one line of dialogue or narration in a scene. Nevertheless, the principle is to remain aware of how parts fit into wholes, even if you are dealing with only a part.

Note that such a literary unit may or may not conform to the chapter and verse divisions in printed Bibles. The unit you delimit may or may not conform to the paragraph or sentence divisions of a printed Bible (though these are more reliable indicators of structure than the chapter and verse divisions). Pay attention to the way your passage is arranged on the page. In poetic portions of the NRSV, for instance, an extra line or two of white space between chunks of text is a deliberate choice of the translators, designed to indicate literary units; though again, not all critics agree about boundaries so you may choose to differ.

Let me offer some examples of the form-content criterion Trible mentioned.

Judges 13–16 contains the story of Samson. In terms of content, we have a clear unit. Chapters 12 and 17 are not about Samson (though on another day, you may want to show the links between Judges 13–16 and its immediate context). But there are formal markers of these boundaries too. Judges 13.1 begins with "Manoah" and "Zorah." Judges 16.31, the final verse of the Samson story, ends with references to "Manoah" and "Zorah." Form, the way that the language is arranged, and content, the actual meaning of the language, cohere.

Let's stir the pot. Judges 13–16 itself can be divided into sections, and here, again, form and content can guide us. Judges

13 is about Samson's birth in terms of content. Formally, too, the final verse of the chapter, v. 31, takes us back to Zorah, where we began in v. 1. This structural device has many names: inclusio, bracketing, enveloping; and it is a trademark of biblical style. You mark the end of something by repeating, whether in continuity or contrast, the beginning. Most biblical stories, on a narrative level, get you back home.

In the above example, the chapter division in our Bible is a reliable guide to the internal structure of the material. But not so for the rest of the Samson story. How is it structured?

Its individual episodes are marked by repetition.

In Judges 14.1, Samson goes to Timnah and "sees" a woman;
in Judges 16.1, Samson goes to Gaza and "sees" a woman;
in Judges 16.4, Samson "loves" a woman in the Sorek Valley.

We have a story with a tripartite structure, like count-less jokes ("Did you hear the one about the Jewish Rabbi, the Catholic priest, and the Protestant preacher who went golfing?") where the pay-off and punch-line occur in the third section.

Consider Exodus 3–4. By content this is the account of God's revelation to Moses on Mt. Sinai/Horeb. But where exactly does it begin and end? Is there something intrinsic to the text that says, "We're at a logical break here; you can stand and stretch you legs"?

The beginning is clear. Exodus 3.1 begins a new scene. But where does it end? This one is not clear-cut so the key for an interpreter is to have a sound reason for making a judgment. For me, the signal given in the text is Exodus 4.20. Verse 3.1 begins with Moses as a goatherd and shepherd, and 4.20 ends the episode by emphasizing that Moses now holds "the staff of God." What does the passage show? Moses ascends the mountain as a herder of small livestock; he descends as a herder of people.

Note here that the word "staff" didn't appear in 3.1, as it did in 4.20, and the word "shepherd" didn't appear in 4.20, as it did (as a verb) in 3.1. The formal boundary is not always indicated by a magic word, and repetition can be of ideas, not simply language.

And sometimes, by Ned, the rascals who translated the Bible into English have obscured the Hebrew original where these structural clues were clearly presented. For instance, I see a literary unit in Exodus 1.8—2.25. In terms of content, this section (which could be divided into smaller units) concerns the Israelites' suffering and God's response. But where can one find a formal, internal guide to structure, which secures our sense that, at some level, Exodus 1–2 is a literary unit? Exodus 1.8 begins the section by talking about a king in Egypt who did not know Joseph. Exodus 2.25 echoes this back. The NRSV mishandles it by translating, "God took notice of them." A better translation of the Hebrew is "but God knew." Pharaoh does not know but God does know. Cut. Scene over.

Or look at 2 Kings 5. By content, this is a single story of Elisha's work in healing Namaan's leprosy. As it turns out, the chapter division coheres with both the form and content. Note how the language of the final verse repeats elements from the initial verse. On a formal level this signals closure. Also, in terms of content, there is a logical, even Newtonian, symmetry to the story. What goes up must come down. Namaan, here a good guy, gets healed of leprosy (or some skin malady) but Gehazi, here a bad guy, contracts it.

Obviously I am showing you examples that work. Not all units of the Bible can be separated so cleanly. But your task, when you examine a passage, is to find its limits by making an argument on the basis of the coherence of form and content.

In both the passages from which you choose one for treatment, the initial boundary is relatively clear while the terminal boundary is not. You are the critic (from the Greek word for "judge") and you must render your judgment on the basis of the interaction of form and content. Even if in some ultimate sense your choice is not the best, at least you have good reasons for your choice.

You are looking for the place in the text where the oral storyteller got a breath or the ancient writer lifted the reed and stretched his or her hand.

4. "Repetition of words, phrases, and sentences."

> As a basic phenomenon in biblical speech, repetition (verbatim and modified) provides the background for discerning structure and meaning.

See the example of Samson and the three women in Judges 14–16.

Or take Jonah 1 where repetition abounds. One example of this is in 1.4 and 1.15. In 1.4, the Lord hurls a great wind on the sea and there is a storm. In 1.15, the Phoenician sailors hurl Jonah into the sea and there is calm.

Now, in the course of your examination of a passage, you will have to decide how the repetition is being used as a marker of structure and meaning. When you actually write your paper, you can explain, by your lights, the significance of the repetition.

Why is repetition so common in biblical style? Because much of the Bible has its roots in oral, not written, discourse. And even the written style of the Bible, in an era early in the history of the alphabet, long before there is widespread literacy, often has the style of oral storytelling. And in oral discourse, speakers must repeat themselves in order to get their point across because the audience cannot turn back the page.

In fact, if you want to get fancy, you can see across vast oceans of the Bible certain themes undulating again and again: creation, chaos, re-creation; home, exile, return. Repetition is a crucial aspect of the biblical style, from the parallelism of a line of Hebrew poetry to the patterns that structure entire books.

5. "Types of discourse."

Note how narration and dialogue interact. Which parts of your unit are each? Is there a pattern in the use of dialogue and narration? Does God speak to the prophet (dialogue), followed by narration, and then the prophet speaks to the king (dialogue), followed by narration? Is there tension or harmony between what is said and what is done? In Jonah 1, in direct speech, God gives a command. Jonah does not respond in speech. Instead he simply does the opposite.

6. "Design and structure."

> Much like a building, an individual text has an overall design and numerous sections. The two interrelate. Describing the architecture is your task. Struggle with how the parts and the whole cohere.

7. "Plot development. Trace the movement of narratives from the beginnings to their ends."

Whether you show your reader this or not, write out for yourself, in phrases or complete sentences, a step-by-step description of what transpires in your text. It is amazing how this simple task can illuminate matters as well as eliminate misreading. Over and over again, whether because we assume we already know what the Bible says or because we lose our concentration or we want to improve the theology of a story, we misread the Bible.

8. "Character portrayals."

Who talks? Who doesn't? Who is named? Who isn't? How do the characters address each other? How does the narrator refer to them? Can you discern social hierarchies among the characters? Who, on the surface, has the power in the story? Who does below the surface? As Trible suggests, "Analyze differences in gender, nationality, and class." If names are given, what do they mean and do those meanings have significance (sometimes they do and sometimes they do not)?

Do any of the characters appear to be "types" (i.e., characters that often appear in stories and about whom the audience and speaker may have shared preconceptions)? Do the characters play against type or conform to expectations? Here, we should also be aware that our cast of typical characters might not be the same or perform the same functions as theirs.

9. Render in diagram form an outline of your passage. "Then describe in clear prose what the structural diagram shows."

10 "Correlate your discoveries."

Think of a way to present your information clearly and persuasively, so that it brings out the meaning(s) you have discerned in the passage.

Some final, more general notes on the paper:

The paper should be no more than 2000 words.

Although in class and in this handout, I often use language informally, compose your paper in your best English style (although without imitating the worst excesses of scholarly jargon and over-writing).

You should do some research but, as you can tell from the above guidelines, most of the work involves your own wrestling with the text.

A final quote from L. Alonzo-Schökel found in Trible:

> With the sweat of your forehead you shall produce fruit.

Share the fruit, not the sweat.

Appendix C

Language, Style, and Citations for Academic Research in World Christianity

Professor Daniel Jeyaraj

LANGUAGE AND STYLE

1. The renewal area courses, such as World Christianity and Global Christianity examine the collective histories, memories, thoughts, struggles, and experiences of non-Western Christians and draw relevant insights for Christian ministry of the students in their Western contexts.

2. Therefore your essay should invariably address at least some aspects of non-Western Christianity and highlight relevant principles for your ministry in your own context. Do not be satisfied with your answers dealing with the questions such as who, what, when, and where of World Christianity and Global Christianity, but emphasize the answers to questions such as *why* and *how*.

3. Your academic paper should be written either from a narrative or a descriptive or an analytical perspective. In every level it should interact, as much as possible, with the primary sources of your chosen theme.

4. Your academic paper should produce either a body of original knowledge or a new interpretation of already available knowledge.

5. Your academic paper should be subject-specific (i.e., pertaining to World Christianity or Global Christianity), and theme-specific (i.e., the chosen topic of your research). It should follow the conventional methods and standards of academic writing, preferably Turabian's style. It should demonstrate high norms of academic honesty and integrity.

6. Avoid all details that do not directly address the chosen theme of the paper. If you have to include secondary details (e.g., titles of a book or an essay, the institution in which the author of your essay worked/works, the honors he/she received, and the like) then place them in the footnotes/endnotes.

7. Your academic paper should incorporate *the findings of at least five or more scholars* who have worked in the field of your chosen theme. Remember that during the 2,000 year history of Christianity numerous scholars have already worked on every major theme that you as a student of this course might wish to write on.

8. Prefer to read the essays that are published either in academic journals or in edited books. These essays will introduce you to a wide variety of scholars, their research findings, and writing styles. Do not quote from popular journals.

9. Your academic paper should not repeat the facts and details found in books and journal articles. What you write and how you interact with your source materials is more important than mere evidence of your reading.

10. Remember that your essay is not about what or how you feel about a particular theme. But it is about how you *interact* with the opinions and concepts expressed in the texts that you have read and examined.

11. Be cautious about anonymous texts that are available Online. Generally, they are substandard. References to these sources will decrease the academic value of your paper.

12. Your academic paper should illustrate how you will relate the new insights that you have gained through this course to your ministerial context. Include course readings and other writings pertaining to this course in making these connections. Therefore let 75 percent of your research paper deal with factual matters, and the remaining 25 percent with the relevance of your research to the context of your ministry. An academic paper without this relevant part will not merit a pass grade!

13. Be careful in acknowledging the source of your knowledge and information and thus avoid every trace of plagiarism. Evidence of plagiarism will have serious consequences. You are responsible for what your paper contains and what it fails to contain.

14. Write your academic essay by using formal language even though at times you may feel uncomfortable with it. Academic essays should avoid colloquialism.

15. Keep the use of either the first or the second person pronouns (i.e., I, we, me, mine, our, you, and your) to the minimum. It is better to use the third person (i.e., he, she, it, they).

16. Use gender-sensitive and gender-inclusive language, clearly highlighting gender identities.

17. Avoid judgmental statements or expressions such as "unfortunately, regrettably" and the like. You can critique an essay of an author; but we are not called to judge the author of the essay.

18. Avoid unguarded generalizations and vague expressions (e.g., "the missionaries," "crusaders," "colonizers," in Africa/Asia/Latin America, and the like). Be specific: specify the name of the missionaries, the identity of the crusaders, by pointing out their nationality, religious or political loyalties, the geographical area of their work, and when they lived.

19. Avoid sweeping statements: Do not write: "All Arabs are Muslims" or "India is a Hindu country." Be specific by reporting that "most Arabs are Muslims. Some Arabs are also Christians." "Most Muslims do not live in West Asia, but in South and Southeast Asia." Qualify your statements and conclusions, and back them up with evidences, preferably from written sources. As you progress in theological and ministerial skills, you may include other sources.

20. Avoid repetitions, colloquialism, wordiness, un-reflected quotes, academic or professional titles of people (e.g., Mrs., Dr., Prof., Rev., and the like), references to classroom lectures, emotional expressions, gender-exclusive language, colonial or ethnocentric words and phrases (e.g., Near East, Middle East, Far East, Old World, New World, Orient, Occident, Minority World, Majority World, and the like), empty words (e.g., few, many, several, all, always, never, everywhere, down through the centuries, all over the world, here and there, on the whole, this is to say . . . , and the like), and ambiguous statements. Be specific!

21. Underline or put in italics all non-English words used in your essay. Then the meaning of a non-English word is explained immediately in the parentheses. For example, the Vedas (religious Scriptures, derived from the Sanskrit *Veda* meaning "spiritual knowledge"); *shoah* (Hebrew word meaning "destruction," and generally used in place of the derogative term *holocaust* or burnt offering).

22. Use active voice more than passive voice. For example, do not write: "Missionaries were sent to India." Write: "The Congregational Church in Boston sent Adoniram Judson and his wife Ann Hasseltine as missionaries to India." Be brief and specific!

CITATIONS

Every student is a learner. As students and learners we depend on the methodologies and several bodies of knowledge generated by other scholars. Christians can draw from their more than two thousand years of collective experiences, thoughts, and expressions. Only in interaction with the concepts, ideas, opinions, hypotheses, interpretations, and findings of other scholars, especially either through affirmation or disagreement or reinterpretation or adapting insights to a new situation, students will be able to create their own knowledge. This is the reason that they should be honest about their sources by citing them in an appropriate manner.

Citations are done in the form of in-text references, footnotes, or endnotes. They enhance and deepen the theoretical orientation and intellectual argument of students. Of several available citing methods four are important: APA-Style,[1] CBE-Style,[2] MLA-Style,[3] and Chicago/Turabian-Style.[4] Andover Newton Theological School recommends for students to use Chicago/Turabian-Style because it allows them to give in footnotes and endnotes additional details that locate the argument of scholars in their context. The first footnote/endnote entry is complete; all subsequent references to this reference are abbreviated. The first line of the footnote/endnote is indented.

---

1. *Publication Manual of the American Psychological Association.* (Washington, DC: American Psychological Association, 2001).

2. *CBE Manual For Authors, Editors, and Publishers.* 6th ed. (Cambridge: Cambridge University Press; 1994).

3. Joseph Gibaldi, *MLA Handbook for Writers of Research Papers.* 6th ed. (New York: Modern Language Association of America, 2003).

4. Kate L. Turabian: *A Manual for Writers of Term Papers, Theses, and Dissertations*, John Grossman and Alice Bennett, eds., 6th ed. (Chicago: University of Chicago Press, 1996).

Two Most Used Citations

From a book:

[1] Gerald H. Anderson et al., eds., *Mission Legacies: Biographical Studies of Leaders of the Modern Missionary Movement* (Maryknoll, NY: Orbis Books, 1994), 3.

Subsequent entry:

Anderson, *Mission Legacies*, 3.

In-text reference:

(Anderson 1994, 3)

From a journal:

[1] Dana L. Robert, "Women in World Mission: Controversies and Challenges from a North American Perspective," *International Review of Mission* 93, no. 368 (2004): 60.

Subsequent entry:

Robert, "Woman in World Mission," 60.

In-text reference:

(Robert 2004, 60)

Bibliographical Entries

Bibliographical entries are arranged in alphabetical order. Remember to refer to the entire length of a journal article (not just to the page referenced in the footnote/endnote).

Anderson, Gerald H., Robert T. Coote, Norman A. Horner, and James M. Phillips, eds. *Mission Legacies: Biographical Studies of Leaders of the Modern Missionary Movement.* Maryknoll, NY: Orbis Books, 1994.

Robert, Dana L. "Women in World Mission: Controversies and Challenges from a North American Perspective." *International Review of Mission* 93, no. 368 (2004): 50–61.

u

A summary of the sixth edition of Turabian-Style   Available Online at http://www.bridgew.edu/Library/turabian.cfm (as of December 22, 2006).

Type of entry	Note Entry Form	Bibliography Form
Book, one author	Daniel A. Weiss, *Oedipus in Nottingham: D. H. Lawrence* (Seattle: University of Washington Press, 1962), 62.	Weiss, Daniel A. *Oedipus in Nottingham: D. H. Lawrence.* Seattle: University of Washington Press, 1962.
Book, two authors	Walter E. Houghton and G. Robert Strange, *Victorian Poetry and Poetics* (Cambridge: Harvard University Press, 1959), 27	Houghton, Walter E., and G. Robert Strange. *Victorian Poetry and Poetics.* Cambridge: Harvard University Press, 1959.
Book, 3+ authors / Book in a series	Jaroslav Pelikan and others, *Religion and the University*, York University Invitation Lecture Series (Toronto: University of Toronto Press, 1964), 109.	Pelikan, Jaroslav, M. G. Ross, W. G. Pollard, M. N. Eisendrath, C. Moeller, and A. Wittenberg. *Religion and the University.* York University Invitation Lecture Series. Toronto: University of Toronto Press, 1964.

Book, no author given	*New Life Options: The Working Women's Resource Book* (New York: McGraw-Hill, 1976), 42.	*New Life Options: The Working Women's Resource Book.* New York: McGraw-Hill, 1976.
Institution, association, or the like, as "author"	American Library Association, *ALA Handbook of Organization and 1995/1996 Membership Directory* (Chicago: American Library Association, 1995), MD586.	American Library Association. *ALA Handbook of Organization and 1995/1996 Membership Directory.* Chicago: American Library Association, 1995.
Editor or compiler as "author"	J. N. D. Anderson, ed., *The World's Religions* (London: Inter Varsity Fellowship, 1950), 143.	Anderson, J. N. D., ed. *The World's Religions.* London: InterVarsity Fellowship, 1950.
Edition other than the first	William R. Shepherd, *Historical Atlas*, 8th ed. (New York: Barnes & Noble, 1956), 62.	Shepherd, William R. *Historical Atlas*, 8th ed. New York: Barnes & Noble, 1956.

Reprint edition	Gunnar Myrdal, *Population: A Problem for Democracy* (Cambridge: Harvard University Press, 1940; reprint, Gloucester, MA: Peter Smith, 1956), 9.	Myrdal, Gunnar. *Population: A Problem for Democracy.* Cambridge: Harvard University Press, 1940. Reprint, Gloucester, MA: Peter Smith, 1956.
Component part by one author in a work by another	Paul Tillich, "Being and Love," in *Moral Principles of Action*, ed. Ruth N. Anshen (New York: Harper & Bros., 1952), 663.	Tillich, Paul. "Being and Love." In *Moral Principles of Action*, ed. Ruth N. Anshen, 661–72. New York: Harper & Bros., 1952.
Electronic document, from Internet	William J. Mitchell, *City of Bits: Space, Place, and the Infobahn* [book on-line] (Cambridge, MA: MIT Press, 1995, accessed 29 September 1995); available from http://www.mitpress.mit.edu:80/City_of_Bits/Pulling_Glass/ index.html; Internet.	Mitchell, William J. *City of Bits: Space, Place, and the Infobahn* [book on- line]. Cambridge, MA: MIT Press, 1995, accessed 29 September 1995; available from http://www-mitpress. mit.edu:80/City_of_Bits /Pulling_Glass/ in-dex.html; Internet.

Encyclopedia, unsigned article	*Collier's Encyclopedia*, 1994 ed., s.v. "Mindoro."	Well-known reference books are generally not listed in bibliographies.
Encyclopedia, signed article	C. Hugh Holman, "Romanticism," in *Encyclopedia Americana*, 1988 ed.	Well-known reference books are generally not listed in bibliographies.
Interview (unpublished) by writer of paper	Nancy D. Morganis, interview by author, 16 July 1996, Fall River, MA, tape recording.	Morganis, Nancy D. Interview by author, 16 July 1996, Fall River, MA. Tape recording.
Newspaper article	"Profile of Marriott Corp.," *New York Times*, 21 January 1990, sec. 3, p. 5.	"Profile of Marriott Corp." *New York Times*, 21 January 1990, sec. 3, p. 5.

Article in a journal or magazine published monthly	Robert Sommer, "The Personality of Vegetables: Botanical Metaphors for Human Characteristics," *Journal of Personality* 56, no. 4 (December 1988): 670.	Sommer, Robert. "The Personality of Vegetables: Botanical Metaphors for Human Characteristics." *Journal of Personality* 56, no. 4 (December 1988): 665–683.
Article in a magazine published weekly (or of general interest)	Robin Knight, "Poland's Feud in the Family," *U.S. News and World Report*, 10 September 1990, 52.	Knight, Robin. "Poland's Feud in the Family." *U.S. News and World Report*, 10 September 1990, 52–53, 56.
Thesis or dissertation	O. C. Phillips, Jr., "The Influence of Ovid on Lucan's *Bellum Civile*" (PhD diss., University of Chicago, 1962), 14.	Phillips, O.C. Jr. "The Influence of Ovid on Lucan's Bellum Civile." .PhD. diss., University of Chicago, 1962.

Students who wish to have additional help in writing may approach either the instructor or the writing tutor.

Appendix D

Research and Writing in Ethics and Congregational Life

Professor Sharon Thornton

FINAL PAPER: ANALYSIS OF AN ETHICAL DILEMMA FROM YOUR MINISTRY SETTING

Review pp. 152–65 of Karen Lebacqz's *Professional Ethics: Power and Paradox*.

Framework includes:

Identifying and accurately describing a specific dilemma requiring the answer to the question: "The right thing to do in this situation is . . . "

- Answering this question will mean defining and interpreting the situation with a view to identifying morally relevant features. This will involve balancing a set of prima facie duties and discerning which duty is most compelling for this situation.

- Part of the discernment will mean paying attention to the role expectations of the profession. In addition it will be important to acknowledge any biases from personal and professional formations you bring to this situation.

- Part of this discernment will involve acknowledging established "rules" that have been designed to guide ethical decision-making. This will involve considering the possible consequences of the decision being considered. It will also involve recognizing the role-activated duties.

- Answering the question, "The right thing to do in this situation . . . " will also involve assessing the character of the professional, in this instance, clergy. The question is not simply what is the right answer to the moral dilemma, but what kind of person is asking the question? It will also mean paying attention to the integrity of the people/person involved in the dilemma—what decision is consistent with their life narrative/s.

- Answering the question will involve paying attention to the structures of power, justice, and liberation.

- Implications: If ethics for ministry is larger than simply the pastor's professional duties, how does one address the requirement for developing "communities of moral discourse?"

Questions to guide your thinking:

1. What is the full configuration of the dilemma?

   Usually consists of a cluster of tangled problems.
   Which problem is weightier?
   One is tempted to respond to symptoms and by doing so, miss the full scope of the dilemma.

2. Who is involved in this dilemma?

   Peers (other clergy or leaders)
   Other professionals
   Parishioners
   General public
   Some combination of the above

Often this points to the difficulty in moving between congregational, community, and professional worlds, each with its own set of values and assumptions.

3. Who has authority? What is the scope of "my" authority? From where is it derived?

This can point to the clergy as an "ethos bearer"—expected to represent the standards and traditions of a particular denomination. This becomes complicated when we remember there are sub-traditions within traditions and different points of view within denominations.

What ethos is being borne into this situation? Does the minister carry her/his family ethos? His/ her community's way of life? The style of a trusted mentor? Etc.

4. What duties do I have to the parties involved?

Confidentiality to my parishioner, client, etc.
Duty of service to my parishioner
Duty of citizenship to the general public
Etc.

5. Where is the conflict of duties that creates the dilemma?

For example, the duty of confidentiality to my parishioner or client would prevent me from divulging information to my peer, whereas the duty to support my peer in his/her work would require that I divulge information relevant to their work.

In most dilemmas, "oughts" collide around issues of doing no harm, doing good, autonomy, etc.

A question becomes: Which principles do clergy generally invoke in difficult situations and are these principles adequate? Are they congruent with the religious communities' orientation? What are the sources for the principles that we apply, either consciously or reflectively?

6. What metaphors and images influence pastoral decision-making?

Here we are probing the influences that lie beneath principles, character, definitions of context, and rational understanding of solutions to human problems. For example, how one perceives God as creator, friend, interventionist, intentionalist, or absent, greatly influences what sort of principles or perceptions will be applied in any given situation.

7. What are the consequences of alternative possible courses of action (usually a harm vs. benefit calculus)?

8. Which factors in the situation are relevant and which are extraneous (and why)?

This is sometimes the hardest to answer. For example, does it make a difference whether something was divulged to you in your office or over coffee in the local coffee shop?

9. How would the dilemma/consequences change if factors x, y, or z were changed?

For example, suppose the parishioner were an adult and not an adolescent; suppose your peer were an alcoholic and not a teetotaler; etc. (Exploring this question often helps get at what is going on in no. 6.)

10. Of the central duties involved in the dilemma, are there grounds for arguing that one is stronger than another?

11. What structural issues impact this dilemma? What are the demands of justice?

12. Are there analogies to the dilemma that might help you sort out the norms involved, and the arguments on behalf of each norm?

This often appeals to ethical images and models and examples of ethical choices in similar situations.

These are not exhaustive questions. They offer ways to begin thinking through the ethical dilemma you are considering so you can argue your case for answering the question, "The right thing to do in this situation is . . . "

CONGREGATIONAL LIFE: GUIDELINES FOR CONGREGATIONAL ANALYSIS: PART I

This is an assignment that will involve you in a comprehensive *description* of your community of faith. In this assignment you are primarily interested in things that will answer questions pertaining to "what, where, when and how." You will look, listen, see, and observe. Talk to folks: church members, visitors, leaders, and professional staff. Examine records such as minutes, reports, advertisements, etc. If you start to wander into the range of "why," stop it! That will be the material for your final reflection paper. While some amount of interpretation is unavoidable, your primary task is to *describe* your community of faith as "thickly" as possible, providing significant details observed within the congregational setting and culture and the various relationships involved. Use some of the research tools provided in *Studying Congregations*, edited by Nancy Ammerman and others. Draw upon course readings, where possible, to inform your analysis.

What is a portrait of congregational life in your community of faith?

1. How does your congregation identify itself in terms of tradition? If related to a denomination, how closely? Describe and substantiate this.

2. Who is your congregation? This will involve you in a demographic study of the congregation: Age of folks, race/ethnicity, gender identification, education, class—income level (Steady over time? New or old wealth?), type of work, etc.? Where do people come from in order to meet together in this particular community of faith?

3. How does your community of faith practice congregational life? What are the programs, activities (formal and informal), and how does it govern itself? Prioritize these and show "artifacts" to substantiate your ordering. Where is there "life?" Where is there "decay?"

4. How does your congregation see itself in terms of being open and inviting? How is it closed and reserved? Who is not there? (Look at your answers to no. 2.) Who is welcomed? Who is ignored?

5. How does your congregation relate with other congregations in its locality?

6. Where is your congregation's "center of gravity"—its focal hub of energy, life, and involvement?

7. Does your congregation view itself as "in the world?" "Apart from the world?" Somewhere in-between? Substantiate your congregation's position.

8. What local, national, and global issues are affecting your congregation? How do you know these are pressing on the congregation?

9. What stories do the members of your congregation tell about themselves?

10. What story would you tell about this congregation: "Once upon a time. . . . And they lived happily (or not) ever after."

CONGREGATIONAL LIFE: GUIDELINES FOR CONGREGATIONAL STUDY PART II: THEOLOGICAL REFLECTION

In your first analysis of your congregation you primarily addressed questions of "what, where, when, and how." This is now the time to begin asking, "Why?" Why do people go to this church? Why is it important for their lives and/or the lives of others? What is the purpose of this church and its ministry? (If you haven't already done so, you might ask some folks these questions.)

H. Richard Niebuhr once wrote: "The purpose of the church is for the increase of the love of God and neighbor?"

Letty M. Russell writes: " . . . the church is a community of Christ, bought with a price, where everyone is welcome."

1. Look at chapter 1 in *Studying Congregations* to help position you for this assignment—particularly pp. 24–38.

You have already done the groundwork, so use the information you have gathered to interpret how your congregation understands itself as church. What is its "indigenous" ecclesiology? (The following questions are suggestive and you are not limited to these specific entry points into your reflection.)

2. Looking at the tradition or denomination that your congregation identifies with, how does your congregation reflect its traditions' views on what it means to be church? How does it differ?

Refer to the data you gathered to illustrate this.

3. How does the way your congregation's self-understanding of what it means to be "church" become reflected in its mission statement (or not) and lived out in its organizational structures and programmatic life? If your congregation's self-understanding of what it means to be church is different from the stated mission statement, what understanding of church is lived out in its organizational structures and programmatic life?

4. How do the demographics related to your congregation reflect (or not) the mission and purpose of the church?

5. Revisit the stories the members of your congregation told about themselves to see if there are Scriptures or sacred texts, symbols, or traditions that come to mind that can

give you clues to your church's deeper understanding of its purpose and mission.

6. Look again at what you identified as your congregation's "center of gravity." Paying attention to this center can provide a way to focus diverse aspects of you congregation in a way that evokes an image or phrase that will give you a "quick grasp" of your congregation's implicit ecclesiology (p. 27, Congregations). Relate the image or phrase to religious themes, stories, and symbols that can illumine the implicit, or "lived faith" of the congregation.

7. What vision of a restored creation/mended world/healed community does your congregation hold? How do you see this being lived by the people?

8. What do you see as a "next step" for this congregation to live more fully and faithfully into a meaningful future?

9. Now that you have closely examined your congregation, try writing a prayer or meditation that reflects your concerns, hopes, appreciation, etc. for this community of people as they continue in the particular ministry that is theirs.

10. Thank you.

Appendix E

Guidelines for Written Assignments in Practical Theology

R. PAZMIÑO

STYLE OR FORMAT

1. Title page included in Turabian style with author's name

2. Title summarizes main idea of paper and is a concise statement

3. All research studies and works are properly cited using Turabian style

4. References are used correctly primarily drawing upon texts and journals

5. Bibliography is in standard Turabian format

6. Writing style, and paragraph structure and development are clear using headings and subheadings to note major points or organization

7. Grammar and syntax are strong and contribute to clarity of style (Remember K.I.S.S.—Keep It Simple Saint—when at all possible)

8. Mechanical aspects of writing (punctuation, spelling, etc.) are strong indicating a spell check and review of the paper before submission

CONTENT OR SUBSTANCE

1. Introduction makes clear the purpose of the paper identifying the topic and an issue, question, or problem of particular interest

2. Introduction states how the purpose will be achieved including the author's position

3. Introduction describes the organization of the paper

4. Major conclusions of the studies, works, and/or insights referred to are relevant to the study or topic

5. There is a clear discussion of the cited research showing its contribution to understanding the topic

6. A summary of major points found in the research is included in the final section of the paper

7. The author includes her/his own conclusions concerning the importance of this topic and its applications to personal and or communal growth and ministry

8. Paper demonstrates understanding of topic with critical and creative thought along with originality

Comprehensive Bibliography

Barth, Karl. *Evangelical Theology: An Introduction.* Trans. Grover Foley. Garden City, NY: Doubleday & Co., 1964.

Clowney, Edmund P. *Called to the Ministry.* Phillipsburg, NJ: Presbyterian and Reformed Publishing, 1964.

Dean, Kenda Creasy, and Ron Foster. *The God Bearing Life: The Art of Soul Tending for Youth Ministry.* Nashville: Upper Room Books, 1998.

Dresner, Samuel H., ed. *I Asked for Wonder: A Spiritual Anthology, Abraham Joshua Heschel.* New York: Crossword, 1995.

Du Bois, W. E. B. *The Souls of Black Folk.* New York: Bantam Books, 1989.

Foster, Charles R., Lisa E. Dahill, Lawrence A. Golemon, and Barbara Wang Tolentino. *Educating Clergy: Teaching Practices and Pastoral Imagination.* San Francisco: Jossey-Bass, 2006.

Fowler, James W. *Becoming Adult, Becoming Christian: Adult Development and Christian Faith.* San Francisco: Jossey-Bass, 2000.

Huebner, Dwayne. Lecture for the course, "Theory of Curriculum Design," Teachers College, Columbia University, New York, NY, November 8, 1978.

Kimelman, Reuven. "Abraham Joshua Heschel: Our Generation's Teacher in Honor of the Tenth Yahrzeit." *Religion and Intellectual Life* 2 (Winter 1985) 17.

Niebuhr, H. Richard, Daniel D. Williams, and James M. Gustafson. *The Advancement of Theological Education.* New York: Harper & Bros., 1957.

———. *The Purpose of the Church and Its Ministry.* New York: Harper & Bros., 1956.

Palmer, Parker J. *To Know As We Are Known: A Spirituality of Education.* San Francisco: Harper & Row, 1983.

Pazmiño, Robert W. *By What Authority Do We Teach? Sources for Empowering Christian Educators.* Eugene, OR: Wipf and Stock, 2002.

Phenix, Philip H. *Realms of Meaning: A Philosophy of the Curriculum for General Education.* New York: McGraw-Hill, 1964.

——. Lecture for the course "Education and the Faiths of Mankind," Teachers College, Columbia University, New York, NY, October 10, 1979.

Spiritual Formation in Theological Education: An Invitation to Participate. Geneva: Programme on Theological Education, World Council of Churches, 1987.

Temple, William. *The Hope of A New World.* London: Student Christian Movement Press, 1941.

Ueland, Brenda. *If You Want to Write.* Saint Paul, MN: Graywolf Press, 1938.

Westerhoff, John H. *Spiritual Life: The Foundation for Preaching and Teaching.* Louisville: Westminster John Knox, 1994.

Zerubavel, Eviatar. *The Clockwork Muse: A Practical Guide to Writing Theses, Dissertations, and Books.* Cambridge, MA: Harvard University Press, 1999.